SELF
CONTAINED

SELF
CONTAINED
Scenes from a Single Life

EMMA JOHN

CCASSELL

First published in Great Britain in 2021 by Cassell,
an imprint of
Octopus Publishing Group Ltd
Carmelite House
50 Victoria Embankment
London EC4Y 0DZ
www.octopusbooks.co.uk

An Hachette UK Company
www.hachette.co.uk

Text copyright © Emma John 2021

Distributed in the US by
Hachette Book Group
1290 Avenue of the Americas
4th and 5th Floors
New York, NY 10104

Distributed in Canada by
Canadian Manda Group
664 Annette St.
Toronto, Ontario, Canada M6S 2C8

ISBN 978-1-78840-342-9

A CIP catalogue record for this book is available from the
British Library.

Printed and bound in the United Kingdom

10 9 8 7 6 5 4 3 2 1

To Geneva and Becki
and Alex and Jenny
and Tessa and Karen
and my cousin Jen.

CHAPTER 1

The house was full of people I didn't know. I didn't know the house that well either.

Laura and Mark had moved into it five years ago and I had been only an infrequent visitor. It was in a remote suburb on the wrong side of the city, a three-change journey that made me feel tired before I'd even left my flat. They had never attempted it in reverse. It was impossible with the kids.

I negotiated a passage through the living room, elbows folded in, lifting my feet to avoid the more sedentary tots. The entrance hall promised breathing space and somewhere to put down the sausage rolls that were threatening to tumble from my paper plate. By the time I reached the doorway, however, a man in a casual shirt and blue chinos was propping himself up against the frame.

I was now obliged to speak to him; turning back or struggling past to sit alone on the stairs would appear rude. So I introduced myself and he bobbed his head, putting his hand to his mouth as he swallowed a piece of cake. 'Hi,' he replied. 'I'm Steve.' I made an over-bright smile, in lieu of a handshake, that pulled at my cheek muscles.

'How do you know Mark and Laura?' I asked.

'Our kids go to the same school. That's one of ours

just there.' He gestured toward a small blonde bundle sitting on a rug swiping at an iPad. Her clothes looked much more expensive than mine.

'Ah,' I said. And then, because my first response didn't seem enough: 'Nice.'

A woman emerged through the muddle of bodies in the next room, wearing the kind of blouse-skirt combo that made me wonder whether I was a real adult. 'Darling, do you have the changebag? Jojo wants to put on his Spiderman outfit.'

'You said to leave it in the car.'

'Well, I haven't got the keys.'

'They're in my jacket.'

'Then can I have them please?' A micro-flicker of irritation passed between them, followed by the keys.

'Sorry, I'm Rebecca, hi.'

'Nice to meet you. I'm Emma.'

'Oh yes, I've heard Laura talk about you – you're an old college friend, right?'

'Yes.' A bubble of gratification worked its way to my brain. I had, family aside, known Laura longer than anyone here.

'We *love* Laura, don't we Steve? They've been such good friends to us since we moved here. And Amy is just adorable, of course.'

I could hear Amy from the kitchen, wailing with the

urgency and modulation of a 1950s nuclear attack siren.

'Shall I go and get Spiderman, then?' Steve took back the keys and trudged to the door, while Rebecca rolled her eyes in the universal signal for what-are-men-like. We settled into small talk, the left-right feint of where I lived and what I did, then the inevitable shot to the body. 'And are you married?'

In the split-second that followed, I rattled through my available responses.

A simple 'No' would sound abrupt and rude, as if I'd taken the question personally or was harbouring a deep hatred for the institution. I tended to save that for people I found really objectionable.

'No, I'm not,' would, in my experience, elicit the question 'Do you want to be?', which I found painfully intrusive. (Older men tended towards the jocular and knowing 'good for you!', and well-meaning marrieds sometimes countered with the wistful-yet-patronizing 'I *miss* being single'.)

Rebecca seemed perfectly pleasant so I went for my softest option: 'No, not yet.' It was too ambiguous, however, and she looked intrigued.

'But you're with someone?'

'No, not yet,' I repeated, with a laugh I hoped would suggest nonchalance at both the question and my relationship status.

It didn't work. A jet of awkwardness had been released and now hung in the air like aerosol spray in a downstairs toilet. Rebecca gave a sympathetic smile and said something about it only being a matter of time, and I nodded encouragingly and told her I was in no rush. 'I'm quite happy with my life,' I reassured her. Making people feel less uncomfortable about my singleness was a skill I had long practised.

And so I allowed Rebecca to tell me how she had been single for the *longest* time before she met Steve, how you just couldn't force these things and it *always* happened when you weren't looking for it, while I patiently waited my turn to explain that I *wasn't* worried, that I *loved* my independence and planned to make the most of it while I still had it. What neither of us said, or even implied, was that it might also be OK to go an entire life without finding a partner at all.

Laura's voice cut through the living room hubbub, announcing cake. I had already started for the kitchen when I was overtaken by a miniature stampede and realized the invitation wasn't meant for me. The kids held their plates above their heads at the tall counter, then walked back to their seats with exaggerated care. It was the most discipline they had shown all day.

During the church service they had hared up and down the aisles, trailed by the occasional father dispatched to

ensure they didn't brain themselves on the end of a pew. When I was a child, church services were choreographed routines that alternated singing with silence. A stern glance from a schoolteacher or a Guide leader or a mother – be it mine or anyone else's – was enough to maintain a respectful hush.

This christening, however, was blessed throughout with the urgently vocalized thoughts and desires of its youngest participants. It was hard to feel spiritual when, with the congregation bent over in prayer, an unmodified voice brayed that it wanted its Star Wars Lego back.

And yet the service had still made me cry. I had developed a Pavlovian response to baptisms. It wasn't the devil-rejecting and the evil-renouncing that got me, or the dunking at the font, but the moments after, when the priest held the baby and thumbed a symbolic cross on its forehead. I only had to start speaking the words 'Fight valiantly. . .' to feel the prickle behind my eyes. The next five minutes of liturgy were always spent clamping my jaw and willing away embarrassing tears, erasing them with a sneaky tissue. By the time the congregation was joyfully welcoming the newcomer into the Lord's family, my voice would be cracking under the strain of concealment.

I hated the thought of being caught crying in church. I knew what people would think. The woman without the

wedding ring was lamenting her childlessness, keening for a baby of her own. How could I explain that this unbidden surge of emotion had nothing to do with the sight of a flailing infant and everything to do with that perfectly constructed moment of community? The promise – fragile as the flame now being gingerly handed to the godparents – of belonging.

And now we were here, in a small garden with a sandpit, where every conversation was fractured with interruption from knee-high invaders tugging at skirts and trouser legs or other halves who 'just need a minute'. I stood in a small horseshoe of first-time parents, caught in a crossfire of due dates and Mothercare wishlists.

'I definitely recommend the Ding-a-Ling-a-sling. The padded flaps are a *life-saver.*'

'Good to know ... what did you do about breast pumps?' I tried to maintain an expression of absorption as they moved on to NCT classes and midwife visits. Laura slipped in next to me. 'God, this must be so boring for you,' she murmured, apologetically. 'Have you seen the others?'

I nodded. It had been more than a year since our little group had been together in the same room but my college friends were still the people I considered myself closest to. Our lives had melted together under the applied heat of higher education and mild depravity, and it was impossible to imagine them ever separating. We might have become

geographically distanced but we were still locked in a foundational molecular bond.

This afternoon, however, our atomic parts were loosely scattered throughout the assembly. Tom and Hywel were talking to a posse of doctors about their respective hospitals. Boring medical chat had been the major drawback of our undergrad life and I avoided it like hepatitis. Ally was commiserating with some women who couldn't believe how often their children needed new shoes.

Jon had found a couple who lived in East Grinstead and was mining them for information on local estate agents – I had hovered on the edge of that conversation for some time before remembering that I was never, ever going to move to East Grinstead. And Ben had foreseen all of this and found a convincing excuse not to be here.

'How are things with you, anyway?' asked Laura. 'What happened with that guy you liked?'

'Oh, you know. Usual story. It turned out I'd read it all wrong and he wasn't really flirting with me after all.'

'The guy whose goodbye hugs lasted a full 60 seconds?'

'That's the one.'

'Ugh. Bet he was just enjoying the attention. Especially from someone as great as you. Guys are the worst.'

'Well, Mark's not *that* bad.'

Laura snorted. 'You don't have to pick up his pants.'

A dad approached with an armful of baby. 'Sorry

Laura, where's your bathroom? This one's leaking...'

Laura led him off towards her cotton wool reserves and I felt for my phone. There was a message from Marisa – *Drinks?* To which I replied: *Yes. God yes.*

Beside me, a burly toddler rushed a smaller one on a tricycle and bundled him off it with the word 'Mine!'.

'That's not very nice, is it?' I said, bending down to his level. 'Don't you think you should say sorry?'

Burly dropped his jaw, scrunched his eyes and screamed as if I'd inflicted bodily violence upon him. Within seconds, a clutch of women had swooped upon the scene.

'What's the matter, darling?'

'Are you hurt?'

While I tried to explain, Burly bawled something indistinct and pointed at the tricycle, which the smaller toddler had been too wary to reclaim. The women looked at me with stark horror, wrapped Burly in unconditional love and told him of course he could play on the trike.

I texted Marisa again. *Now?*

I was glad I had dressed up for the christening. The bar Marisa had chosen was artfully distressed but the people inside it were not. Usually I hated showing up at a place without knowing anything about it – without, to be honest, having chosen it myself, after considerable internet research and a meticulous winnowing of multiple options.

But I knew that I could always trust Marisa's taste.

'How was Laura?' she asked, as we were directed to a booth. The banquette was so tight to the table we had to fold ourselves into L-shapes as we made our approach.

'She's OK, I think. I didn't get to talk to her that much.'

'Did little Sam behave himself for the vicar?' Marisa had never met either little Sam or Laura but she had an extraordinary memory for the peripheral details of other people's lives and could show a genuine interest in those she didn't know. It was a trait that never ceased to impress me.

A waitress came to take our order and we chose two of the wildest-looking cocktails on the menu. 'Should we get some snacks?' I said, knowing that the answer would be yes and that by the time the bill came, we would have spent as much on some bread, olives and chicken liver parfait as on a full-blown meal. But snacks always sounded like an economical move, and when I did ultimately reel into a chicken shop on my way home, the alcohol in my stomach crying out for the companionship of some filthy fried drumsticks, I would already have forgotten the cost of the olives.

Marisa asked the waitress for her recommendations. A vote for the calamari turned into a discussion about the difference between squid and octopus and soon Marisa had elicited that our waitress once worked on yachts in the Mediterranean and planned to get back there some day if

she could. One of the things I enjoyed most about going out with Marisa was how easily she made conversation with people she'd just met. It came as naturally to her as her generous smile or the Kiwi vowels that she always claimed – incorrectly – to have lost since she moved to Britain.

Even after a decade of living in London, Marisa treated the city as a foreign adventure and approached its citizens with a warmth and curiosity that made her instantly likeable. Nowhere was off limits or intimidating when you were with her because she was never striving to fit in. Her enthusiasm to learn about random strangers was entirely genuine, and under her influence I found myself becoming more interested in them, too – or at least less resentful of their presence and more patient with their life stories.

We had met a year ago. My flatmate was leaving to move into her own place and I couldn't afford to pay the mortgage alone. I had bought the flat in the mid-2000s; my parents had helped with a deposit on the understanding they would get their money back when I eventually married and halved my worldly goods and liabilities with a husband. It was a compact two bedroom at the top of an Edwardian terraced house and three flights of stairs but, as the estate agent had said, perfect for a couple starting out. My mother assumed it was only a matter of time before the dinky second bedroom became a nursery, whereas I had always pictured it as a book-lined study

with a daybed for out-of-town guests who missed the last
train home.

Until then, however, I needed someone to share the
bills with. I was in my thirties, I had a newspaper job and
a decent salary and a series of social rounds that inevitably
emptied my bank account by the third week of every
month. Perhaps I could have indulged less and stayed
home more but then, I reasoned, what would be the point
of living in London at all? After the tortured striving of
my twenties – scrambling up the sides of a slippery pit of
professional anxiety – wasn't it time to enjoy some of the
fruits? The thought of living alone, bored with my own
company, had never appealed to me anyway.

So I posted the vacancy on a website and invited each
of the respondents over to look at the flat; Marisa was the
only one to refuse. 'How about we meet up for a drink
somewhere instead?' she wrote. 'There's no point seeing
the room unless we think we're actually going to get
along.' This made her sound so much wiser and classier
than me that I immediately agreed.

A few days later, we sat down in a pub for a couple
of pints and what we described ever after as the greatest
first date of all time. Rarely had anyone made me feel so
comfortable so quickly: 'How was *your* day?' she asked, as
if we were old friends meeting up at the end of our shifts.
She didn't tell me her life story or ask dull questions about

how many siblings I had. She did offer me a foolproof recipe for blondies and show me the scar she'd got from a high-speed bicycle crash.

I never registered the exact nature of the things we had in common or why she seemed such a kindred spirit. I barely even noticed the tiny diamante nose stud or how she managed to bunch her long hair into the kind of cool, silky mess that looked like an A-lister's gym selfie. I was, however, aware of how much I was laughing and how when *she* laughed, she leaned her head back as if she were making more space to enjoy the joke.

It quickly became apparent that my flat wasn't right for her – the room was too small and she had pieces of furniture that would never make it up the back-breaking staircase. She shrugged it off and stayed for another drink, during which we investigated our relationships with our mothers, our thoughts about religion and our favourite uses for gin. When we discovered our birthdays were two days apart, she groaned. 'I'm gutted I'm not moving in. We'd throw *such* a good party.' I told her I was having a few friends over for a barbecue in the garden at the weekend. She said she would come, and she did.

From then on, Marisa took up the role of my gamest friend. We established a habit of evenings out during which we indulged each other's best and worst excesses. I liked old-world glamour and she liked hipster chic; together

we pinballed between speakeasies and hotel bars as if we were sponsored by Diageo. We became each other's excuse for extravagance and blew our pay cheques on many a 'special occasion' joint that others might have saved for the next job promotion or the arrival of their decree absolute.

This was how I had often hoped my thirties would be. My social life had finally attained the level of sophistication I aspired to – unlike the frenzied gargle of my college days or the fretful outings of my twenties, always riddled with the fear that a better night could have been had at a different location or with other friends. Marisa and I navigated our way through the city's endlessly reconfigured drinking terrain with the assurance of veteran explorers, happiest in unfamiliar territory, hunting for new experiences.

I liked the person I was with Marisa far more than I liked the one I was at home. My new flatmate was not working out; she was almost ten years younger than me, a recent arrival in the city with an urgency to imprint herself that I thoroughly understood and an abrasive streak she had hidden well when we originally met. My cowardly personality shied away from open rows and, in the months that followed her moving in, the little flat became a staging ground for passive-aggressive warfare.

Our conflict peaked in the winter, when the hundred-year-old brickwork failed to provide much insulation. Skirmishes were fought over who was causing draughts

by leaving the doors open and a long-running hostage situation developed over an oil heater I had bought from Argos. Home ceased to be somewhere I could rest or relax, and I didn't feel particularly at peace with myself either. None of this had brought out my best side and the only way I could reconcile how poorly I was behaving to a person I was living with was to tell myself that I deserved whatever discomfort it brought. My penance, therefore, was to constantly forgive and continually endure.

Marisa, meanwhile, was a steadfast reminder that I led an enviable life. With her, I wasn't a psychological weakling or a vicious landlady or a leftover damsel waiting to be rescued by romance. When I waved over a bartender and ordered our martinis – mine extra dry, hers dirty as a used dishcloth – I felt like my own hero. All futures remained open to me: fame, fortune or grand passion.

Whenever there was somewhere I wanted to go – a film, a concert, an art exhibition – Marisa was my first call. She became so recognizable as my plus-one that a gay friend who worked in PR and regularly invited us to his bands' gigs assumed she was my girlfriend. I only realized this after I told him one night that I'd never read any of Vita Sackville-West's poetry and he boomed: 'What kind of lesbian *are* you?' I never bothered to correct him. It reflected pleasingly well on me that anyone would think I could land a Marisa.

I wished I'd met her far earlier in our London lives, back when my contacts book couldn't keep up with my need for companionship. I had not learned, at this time, that Facebook was a terrible place to post about your spare ticket to *Mamma Mia* because the sad-face emojis from everyone you knew explaining that they were already busy would be a very public stamp of loserdom.

If I had known Marisa in my twenties, I reasoned, we would now have the kind of recklessly loyal best-friendship known to female New Yorkers in film and TV, the leave-it-all-on-the-dancefloor, let-it-all-out-in-the-toilet-cubicle relationship that ran around Manhattan in stilettos and collapsed back home with its face in a jar of peanut butter. But it was too late for that; Marisa already had her own support network, including a best friend, Zoe, with whom she had now found a place to live.

And so Marisa was just my going-out friend. Sometimes when I suggested a movie, she had already seen it with Zoe and Zoe's boyfriend Dave, or else they were all feeling broke and Marisa would apologetically decline: 'Zoe and I are going to stay home and cook tonight.' I had only met Zoe a couple of times but I was already jealous of her, and the way she managed to wear her T-shirts so carelessly over her black jeans or raise one eyebrow to convey devastating irony.

It was Zoe who had tipped off Marisa about this bar,

having read about it in a magazine the day before. It struck me, after an afternoon observing the glacial movement of my friends' married lives – the crawling narrative of school years and career advancement – how sparklingly nimble ours felt by contrast. Nothing could have tempted me to trade the possibility of a spontaneous midweek happy hour for the regularity of a Saturday morning supermarket shop.

We sat in our booth dipping crispy squid in a slick of something outrageously garlicky and making over-loud groans of pleasure while Marisa told me about her latest meet-up with Vish. Vish was a former colleague with whom she had unmistakeable chemistry but who stubbornly refused to act on it. They would talk for hours, sharing their deepest thoughts and fears in the manner of soulmates. Then, as they stumbled into the street at closing time, he would give her a meaningful hug, tell her she was one of his closest friends and announce that he was heading in the opposite direction.

I recognized this behaviour; the same thing had happened to me enough times to know this was never going to have a happy ending. 'What is *wrong* with this guy?' I said, with automatic outrage. 'He's *clearly* a total *idiot*.' But underneath the righteous indignation on my friend's behalf, I felt a thrum of something else: a secret, suppressed delight. I knew it was wrong but

I couldn't deny the low-level pleasure in discovering that someone as obviously great as Marisa was stalling with a guy.

This was not the first time that I had experienced irresistible relief on hearing the stories of other women's failures with men. It wasn't that I wanted them to be unhappy – not really, not in the long-term – but their woes did bring me a temporary release from the constant contemplation of my own inadequacies.

They were also some of the times I felt I could understand other women best. I was rarely electrified by the vicarious spark of someone else's romantic obsession. I didn't dissolve at their melty-eyed sharing of a sonogram. However, tell me about the brutal disappointment of a guy who liked you, but not quite enough, and you'd found something I could hum along to. I knew that tune well, from the repeated motif of missed moments and agonizing non-happenings, to the internal bassline moan of why-aren't-I-his-type?

'Do you think I should have just grabbed him and kissed him?' asked Marisa.

'Sounds like you'd have terrified him if you did. If he can walk away from a woman like you, he's clearly got trouser problems.'

'But then why does he spend so much time with me?'

My explanation failed all rules of logic but it was

delivered with enough emotion that it didn't matter: 'Because *you're* amazing and he knows deep down that he doesn't deserve you!'

Marisa sighed. 'He *doesn't* deserve me, does he?'

'No, he doesn't. And your life is far better without him slowing you down.'

We clinked our glasses and cheersed our independence. An outer ripple of relief lapped at my subconscious. I had lost enough good single friends to the blackout zone of serious commitment already.

My flatmate gave me a month's notice of her intention to leave and the siege lifted overnight. Now that we both knew the situation was temporary, we suddenly found it perfectly natural to be kind and our consideration of each other's comfort knew no bounds. She cooked me breakfast; I was happy to watch her choice of TV. The day she moved out, we carried her boxes and bags down to her dad's car together and I sprang back up the stairs.

Our tiny acts of aggression and the disproportionate pain they inflicted had been too ridiculous and shameful to share widely; I had not admitted my role in them to anyone other than my sister. She suggested I think twice before inviting another stranger to live with me.

'Why don't you wait till you find someone you know a bit better?' she said.

'Because everyone I know already has someone they live with.'

'You could afford to live alone for a bit. Especially if you weren't out every night.'

'And never see my friends?'

'Ugh, London people. What's wrong with going round someone's house and eating pizza?'

Kate was two years younger than me but had assumed the role of older sister ever since our late teens. I listened to her advice grudgingly and then, as I almost always did, I took it.

In the pause before committing to anyone new, I decided it made sense to repaint the empty bedroom. Decorating was one of many activities that seemed achievable – even fun – in the abstract but which I usually regretted the moment I was irrevocably committed. Other items on this list included clubbing, strategy-based board games and swimming, which I only remembered how much I despised when the sole of my foot made contact with a wet changing room floor.

I allocated a weekend for my redecorating project, then spent the entire Saturday morning in the aisles of the DIY shop, dithering over brush bristle types and paint roller widths. Without a car of my own, I struggled home on the bus, the heavy tins of paint cloaked in my jumper and jacket after the first driver had spotted them among my

bags and refused to let me on. I climbed the three flights to my front door, realized I'd forgotten dust sheets and went straight out again.

It was almost early evening when I was finally ready to begin painting. There had been a third trip to the shops when, after watching a short YouTube tutorial, I understood that I was supposed to have prepared the walls with something called sugar soap. And then a fourth when I decided the task required emergency chocolate. It was possible I should have quit while I was behind, especially given the heightened state of stress and fatigue under which I was now operating. But once the walls were sponged down and ready for action I felt a strange obligation towards them.

With no one around to dissuade or direct me, I filled a paint tray and loaded up the roller. The first thrust triggered a backspray of vinyl matt across my face and the glasses I was wearing upon it. Some say there is a state of flow inherent to manual pursuits, a hypnotic effect that encourages a mindful calm, and it is true that you can't act out your anger with a roller brush (at least, not without splattering yourself). That night was my proof, however, that you can both paint yourself into a corner and decorate yourself into a depression. The moon was high outside the window by the time I gave up. I threw myself into bed without showering, arms covered in crispy white speckles.

I woke to the dismal thought that I had to wrestle with the roller all over again, at least twice more. Then I remembered the existence of skirting boards and door frames and burst into tears. All that sandpapering! A primer *and* undercoat! Not to mention the gloss paint, a substance I could no more handle than I could nitroglycerine. No masking-tape barrier I built had ever kept it contained. My hallway carpet still bore the stain from my last attempt to touch up some woodwork.

But now I'd started the process there was no escape and no rescue team on its way. If there was one thing that sucked about being single in your thirties, it was the crappy jobs you couldn't expect anyone else to help you do. A decade ago, a painting party was a fun excuse for a hangout and making house was still a novelty. These days, everyone had enough DIY – and life – troubles of their own.

By Monday evening, I had reached a state of hopelessness; by Thursday, I was convinced I was trapped forever in this purgatory of half-finished home improvement. I had unwittingly tramped Antique Cream across my floors and the dust sheets trailed sorrowfully into the hallway, unsure whether they were supposed to be hiding the paint-prints or preventing more. Even with all the windows open – admitting a contemporary symphony of traffic, pavement confrontations and night-time helicopter visits – the fumes preferred to hang around

inside. Which of the two was causing my headaches and keeping me awake at night became an intractable puzzle.

It was on the Friday afternoon that Marisa's text arrived: *Drinks?*

By now, the concept of putting on a skirt and mascara seemed to belong in the realms of science fiction. I would surely never hold an Old Fashioned again.

Wish I could, I replied. *Out of funds, probably forever. Flatmate left and have stupidly attempted to spruce the spare room solo. If you haven't heard from me in a month, please send police to remove my turps-addled body.*

Fifteen seconds later, the phone rang.

'Mate,' she said, 'why didn't you tell me?'

'About my flatmate? Or my redecorating disaster?'

'Both! Are you OK?'

I said I was fine, even though I wasn't, because a voice in my brain warned me that you weren't allowed to be this pathetically miserable about DIY.

'I'll come round and help you tomorrow,' said Marisa. 'It'll be fun.'

She showed up the next morning with a plastic bag containing a selection of paintbrushes, plus a French stick and a giant wedge of cheese she'd brought for our lunch. She was, inevitably, both more competent and more careful than me, but even my brushwork seemed to improve with her around and time slipped by in easy increments.

I didn't dare tell my friend how blissful it was to have her alongside me or how, in the moment she offered to come over, I had felt sluice gates open and a cascade of hopefulness rush in. I did know, already, that whenever anyone admired the room, I would make a point of saying that Marisa and I had painted it together. And I suspected that this wasn't the last thing she would help me fix.

Occasionally we took a break and paused at the window, looking out over the garden. It was an uninteresting stretch of grass with one magnificent feature: a horse chestnut tree whose upper branches reached up to the top of the house. Marisa got excited when she spotted a couple of green parakeets hanging out there. I couldn't fathom what a pair of exotic birds was doing in my garden but I liked to see them, livening the place up with their Granny Smith plumage and rosy pink beaks. There were enough damn pigeons in the world already.

CHAPTER 2

I woke early on the day of my sister's second wedding.
Lying carefully still, eyes on the ceiling, I waited until
I heard a tiny crumple of movement next to me to tell me
that Kate was awake. Then I rolled over onto my right side
and smiled.

'You're getting married today.' My voice sounded a
little tight with excitement.

'I know.'

'Again.'

Kate lay on her back, hands clasped prayer-style over
the duvet. 'What's the time?'

'Six-thirty.'

'Oh. We should probably try to go back to sleep.'

'Yeah.'

When the alarm went off an hour later, Kate was not in
the room. I heard three bleats from the kettle downstairs,
begging someone to validate its good work. There was
a rumble of bodies, too, and I remembered that Robert,
Kate's best friend, had also stayed the night. Then
I thought of something else and refocused my hearing on
the window. Slow, regular taps. It was raining.

I dragged myself down to the lounge where we had,
thankfully, had the foresight to remove the leftover

takeaway and ice-cream cartons the night before. Robert was already in there, bright and cheery and ready to be helpful. I nodded at him and went to make some toast. Kate stood in the kitchen in a dressing gown.

'Do you want breakfast?' I asked.

'I've already had some. I'm going in the shower now, then you can have yours. Dad texted, there are roadworks between here and Dunstable and he has no idea how long it could take to get there so we've got to leave at 9.30.' Her voice had lost the sleepy tinge of an hour ago. It had also lost the girlishness of when we giggled ourselves to sleep the night before. Instead, it assumed the serious and vaguely menacing edge it had learned from our mother. 'So you'll be ready at 9.15, right?'

This all seemed a bit much for a wedding that was taking place in the next town over at midday, but Kate hated rushing. She was, for instance, a stickler for being at airports the full three hours early. My inclination to leave as late as possible – born of a deep aversion to wasting a single productive moment of my life, particularly on any activity as dull as waiting – meant that this was a regular bone of contention between us.

The problem was, as motivated as the day should have made me, I found it hard to work to someone else's deadline, especially my sister's and particularly in the morning. It took an hour and a half for me to wake up

on a normal day. Until mid-morning, my brain seemed to operate under a thick layer of insulation that restricted the tempo at which my limbs would operate. You could shout at me as much as you wanted, I simply wasn't capable of moving the shower puff over my body any faster or chewing down my toast with the same gusto as the rest of my speed-eating family.

And so, at 9am, when I had only just sat down in front of the mirror with the curling tongs, Kate had already put up her hair and done her make-up and been secured into her dress with every kind of fastener short of staples, all without the help of her chief bridesmaid. Alison, Kate's other bridesmaid, was now reassigned to my hair, while the bride became increasingly stressed about our departure time – which she constantly reiterated from the doorway – and her own up-do, which wasn't as good as the one she'd done in practice.

Dad arrived and packed the car while I was still applying eyeliner. A swirling wind blew rain in multiple directions but he had worked out a three-brolly system that could get Kate dryly down the drive and into the car with a fourth person holding her train. Once we were in our seats – Alison next to me in the back, trays of flowers across our laps – the grimness of the weather could no longer be denied. Great globules of water hurled themselves on the windscreen and grey clouds hunched unbroken to the

horizon. There would be no outdoor picnic, no games of giant Jenga. Whether the early evening hog roast would survive was beyond our technical knowledge.

For a moment, there was silence, the silence of four individuals battling their own nerves and disappointments. Then Dad turned on the stereo and from it emerged a jingling kids' tune sung by the twee pairing of Morris and Dorris, magic hamsters from a storytelling tape that had accompanied our family on car holidays when we were little. 'I thought you might like it for your Something Old,' said Dad.

The previous day's wedding had been the legal one, in the tiny village church just over the bridge from my parents' house. Kate had been insistent that this was not the *real* wedding, and it was, originally, to take place in a registry office because Justin didn't believe in God anyway. But then he'd seen the church, and it was charming, and Kate had ended up with a separate legal-wedding dress and a service attended by close family and a champagne barbecue in the garden. I had played everyone down the aisle on my violin, punched out a couple of hymns on the piano and sung a Delibes duet with one of Kate's actress friends.

Today we were headed to a disused airfield and a marquee filled with almost everyone that Kate and Justin knew, which was, it turned out, a lot of people. The bridal party arrived still enclosed in our umbrella shield, where

we huddled until it was each of our turns to walk up the aisle, keeping the bride and dress number two hidden for the big reveal.

I had been there when the dress was found; it had presented itself, with exquisite timing, at the end of an afternoon shopping safari through some of Bedfordshire's minor outposts. These tiny towns always seem to come with their own bridal shop and we decided to visit the one on the high street of a place where Kate and I had spent our earliest years, before our parents had moved us to Luton. It was in a brief row of shops that included an ironmonger, a newsagent and a post office.

When we were little, the sequinned white gowns had always caught our eyes, and we would pause solemnly at the window, pointing out the ugliest. As grown ups, we knew it wasn't right to be judgemental of other people's tastes, so we were careful to pluck each other's sleeves and pull our disgusted faces when the owner wasn't looking. Then Kate had put on The Dress and we'd quickly sobered up. She was transcendent, even pinched together at the back with bulldog clips that gave her the spine of a stegosaurus. I felt a bolt rip through my heart and wondered if it was OK to actually be in love with your sister.

I knew that not everyone felt for their sibling as fiercely as I felt for mine. Laughing with Kate was different to laughing with anyone else I knew. We could reduce each

other to heaving helplessness, could cause each other spasmic pain, with nothing more than an oblique reference to something daft our mother had said several years ago. And there were moments, slumped on sofas watching American sitcoms, when I would catch a side-glance of her face – the one I teasingly called a moonface for its cartoon-like roundness – and think how beautiful it was, and feel a lump in my throat.

But I had been a terrible big sister when we were kids and the guilt of that had only grown in recent years. I hated it when our parents dusted off funny anecdotes of the trouble I'd caused then blamed on my innocent sibling, or the racketeering scheme I had run to 'look after' Kate's pocket money. I dreaded the incriminating photos of games I'd invented requiring a six-year-old Kate to put herself in physical jeopardy, or a nine-year-old one to eat a teaspoon of butter or mustard. The idea that my little sister had willingly participated in all of these – had wanted to be with me, even as she was getting abused – could not be thought of too carefully or it threatened to break my heart.

We became true friends when I went away to university; in my independence, Kate found hers. Our separate identities finally established, we boomeranged back towards each other, grateful for the familiarity of a mind that worked so similarly to our own. Even the circumstances of our lives often seemed to run in parallel.

Many a phone call had pepped us both up to take a stand with our annoying bosses or helped us past a hopeless crush by hearing how tragic the other one's sounded.

So I had expected to feel something at my sister's wedding, but nothing – not even the practice run at the village church – had prepared me for the moment I made my own procession down the aisle. I managed two steps before the emotion rushed to meet me and my body moved as if I were battling wind resistance. I sucked down air to stop myself from crying and later discovered that every photograph of my solo run had cruelly captured my O-shaped mouth.

If the feelings I was experiencing had names, it was hard to identify them beneath the din of my insides clanging against each other. Joy, I recognized, and gratitude, delivered in an envelope of pure adrenalin. But there were other, subtler shades that went unrecognized and I felt, not for the first time in my life, that the vocabulary I had was utterly inadequate for the task and I could do with an emotional thesaurus to understand myself better.

It was hard, as the ceremony proceeded, to concentrate on what the vicar was saying. At least I wasn't missing anything I hadn't heard 24 hours before. Kate, though – Kate was transformed. Was it the train on her dress that gave her a majesty that I found frankly unnerving? Or the fact that her unusual elegance was being reflected back at

her by hundreds of admiring eyes? Whatever it was, she had ceased to be the sister I knew and become some multi-dimensional version whose every facet of her being shone simultaneously, a diamond blinding its wearer.

There were nearly three hundred people in the marquee, a combination of mine and Kate's limitless extended family and her new husband's gift for networking. People had brought their own picnics, giving the whole affair the vibe of a local fete. Instead of a three-tier wedding cake, there was a table of home-baked efforts to be judged by the bride and groom, and the afternoon was punctuated with performances from their friends – the talent bar comfortably high, since Kate had trained in musical theatre and Justin ran a jazz and blues club.

I was happy to drift between the various clusters; it is a particular privilege of a bridesmaid, and a chief one at that, to be able to attend a conversation only as long as it is interesting to her and to excuse herself the moment she tires of it. Everyone assumed I had duties, but with Justin's supremely competent bar manager running the event there was little to do and so I flitted around the tent, grazing from other people's charcuterie selections and bathing them in my radiant happiness by way of recompense.

I felt a little like a celebrity, the way even people from Justin's side of the aisle that I'd never met before knew who I was, the fact that my brief visit with them could elicit

their best smile. Among my own relatives, the effect was heightened; I had never received so many compliments, from my shoes to my hair to my figure. Did I really look that hot, I wondered, or was this wave of appreciation partially triggered by the fact that I was at my sister's wedding without a partner of my own?

Next to the cakes were piles of fortune cookies, although I knew better than to bother breaking one open. When they had been preparing to move in together, Kate had told Justin that on their first night she wanted to eat Chinese takeaway sitting on the floor surrounded by their packing boxes, the way that Americans did in the movies. Justin had arranged for Kate's fortune cookie to have a proposal inside. Unfortunately, a bespoke order had to come in bulk and now he had 2,999 cookies containing the non-transferable message: '*Kate will you marry me?*'

When I first heard of Justin, he was a guy who flirted with my sister but refused to see it through, making him officially a Bad Thing. The fact that she was smitten before she even met him didn't help; Kate had fallen for descriptions of the man as reported by their mutual friends, for his filmmaking CV and his musical passions. When he turned out, in person, to be tall and funny and protective and wildly sociable, she didn't stand a chance.

I kept my distance and shelved him in the special limbo that women keep for men who may destroy their

best friends' hearts. By the time the two were officially dating, our parents had already met Justin; the first time I encountered him, at a family dinner, they were treating him like a son-in-law and passing him the mashed potato (annoying, as it was my favourite, made just for me because no one else in the family ate it). There were pink spots of pleasure on my father's cheeks; I had never seen him look so delighted with anyone.

It also annoyed me that Justin was tall, broad-shouldered and confident. Ours had always been a female-dominated house – our father was the quiet one – and Kate's boyfriend seemed to have found his place in it a bit too easily. He had opinions too and, even though he didn't necessarily share them publicly, I heard them second-hand through my sister and was increasingly aware of the weight they were given.

But really, it annoyed me most that Justin was clearly Kate's soulmate. My sister had other best friends and I had never perceived them as a threat, but now she had connected with someone in an entirely new form of attachment. Until Justin, I had been Kate's bottom line, her last line of defence, someone who listened to her when no one else understood. Kate was still that person to me – the person to whom I took the feelings I couldn't explain or the random thoughts that no one else would be interested in. But I was no longer Kate's person.

One evening after their engagement, it came to me with unusual clarity that I had a decision to make. Kate had gone to the kitchen to get the tiramisu and Justin was asking me about various mundane aspects of my London life that I knew could not possibly interest him. But he was asking anyway, out of kindness and with a certain determination to break through the invisible barrier he kept coming up against. In that instant, I realized that I could decide the future of our relationship. Either I continued to see him as Kate's soon-to-be husband and an accessory to my sister's life or I went all in and chose to love him as a brother.

I made the right decision.

I knew it for sure at the first wedding as the three of us walked the couple of hundred metres from the churchyard to my parents' cottage, pausing on the bridge together to take in the little canalside garden with its homemade bunting strung along the fence and the aunts and uncles gathered with glasses of fizz in their hands. It was Kate and Justin's day, of course, but somehow it had felt like a moment to celebrate my own past and future, too.

After we had toasted and eaten, I went inside to make Justin a coffee, only I forgot to boil the kettle and served my new brother-in-law his strong black coffee stone cold. He had teased me mercilessly and called me Sis, and later, when Kate took selfies of the three of us and I overheard an

uncle call us the Three Musketeers, I knew my world had not shrunk but grown.

Today, I watched them from further away, smoothly bisecting the tent like figure skaters, each arcing their own way for a spell, then circling inevitably back together. Kate had encouraged me to invite whoever I wanted to the 'real' wedding and Marisa, who had been visiting her parents in New Zealand, had arrived in a taxi straight from the airport. Despite 22 hours of accumulated flight time, she had immediately and voluntarily taken on the role of assistant to the chief bridesmaid, refilling my champagne glass with the shimmering discretion of a Mayfair valet.

At one point, she whispered in my ear that an over-excited guest was having a little puke in the posh portaloos and was, to put it politely, ready to go home. 'You don't need to do anything,' she told me. 'Your cousin Karen's looking after her.' Karen was often the designated driver in these scenarios; she'd been teetotal since her early twenties, when it became apparent that alcohol could trigger her epilepsy. Karen had been the first to hug me and my sister at the end of the ceremony, and when Karen said I looked gorgeous, I knew it wasn't a piece of pity praise.

Karen was ten years older than me. She had been a favourite babysitter when Kate and I were little – ebullient, kind and mischievous enough to indulge us in late nights we weren't supposed to have and TV shows

we weren't supposed to see. Through our teens and into our twenties, Karen had become a wonderful resource for the kind of things we didn't want to ask our mother about, particularly boys.

I still loved to talk to her about what I thought of as the 'squashy' problems of life – the ones that no one could resolve for you, like where my career was going or whether I'd be better off blonde. We would sit in the living room of the house Karen shared with her mum and together we would take the thing that was bothering me and give it a good hard squeeze. Its nature might not change but it always felt good to see it bent out of shape for a while. But Kate saw more of Karen than I did these days; they lived in the same town and I suspected that our cousin had spent some time in the navigator's seat when Kate started dating Justin.

Karen and I were the only adults from my mother's vast family tree who remained single, a particular accomplishment given that several of the branches had multiple marriages, and even second cousins who had been born when I was a teenager were now popping out their own progeny. And yet I never thought of my singleness as in any way similar to my cousin's. Karen and her mother had been housemates for a couple of decades now, an arrangement that suited them nicely – they were both gregarious women who loved having each other to

talk to and understood the other's foibles – and aside from some early exploratory adventures, Karen seemed to have resisted romantic relationships.

She had spoken to me at times of needing to feel in control of her body and I guessed that my cousin had in some way discounted herself from the 'regular' course of life because of her epilepsy. Instead, Karen had chosen a path of abstinence, populated with numerous pen pals who – and this I knew, because I had seen the letters – adored both her witty prose and her pretty wisdom. I loved Karen but I didn't see myself becoming her. Whether it was born of frailty or conviction, Karen's commitment to her unchanging trajectory made me feel that we must be made of very different stuff.

It was nearly time for the speeches; the rain had lightened then lifted and the hog roast was back on. In the meantime, it seemed our mother's hostess genes had distracted her from sitting down to her own picnic and an emergency signal reached me, through back channels, that someone really had to get Christine to eat. I found her in the middle of the marquee, giddily broadcasting information about yesterday's exclusive event. Her voice was transmitting an impressive 50 per cent further than its usual, considerable range, holding her audience captive very much in the hostage sense.

I led her gently by the hand towards a coolbox.

'Have a pork pie,' I said, popping it from the plastic tray and pressing the frigid pastry into my mother's palm. Mum giggled like she was Shirley Temple.

'Oh dear, have I been naughty?'

'No, you're just a bit over-excited.'

'I *am* excited!' sang the mother of the bride, to whatever audience she thought she had left. 'I'm high as a kite!'

'Well, you're definitely high.' I located a Tupperware box of chicken satay skewers. 'Try one of these too. Just don't wave it around. Or stab yourself.'

'Yes daughter.' More giggles. 'She's feeding me!' she announced. 'They *do* take care of me, my girls. I'm so proud of them!'

I replaced her wine glass with a plastic tumbler of water and let her loose again. Not long after, I overheard Mum telling one of Justin's elderly relations how she had always said that Kate would marry the first man she fell in love with. I had heard this observation before and tensed for what came next.

'The other one ... well, we knew she was going to play the field.'

My mother had shared this opinion with plenty of people, most of whom, I suspected, cringed with the same quiet embarrassment that I did. 'You should see the way she shops!' Mum would say. 'She'll see something she wants in the very first store but she can't buy it until she's dragged

you through every place in the shopping centre, to be sure. Then she goes back and buys the first thing she saw!'

This piece of hack psychology irritated and bemused me. What irritated me was that it made me look bad, and what bemused me was that it wasn't even true. Well, the shopping part was fair. I did take a perfectionist approach to the art of purchasing and was more afflicted than most with the fear of buyers' regret. But the idea that I had extended the same methodology to my love life was laughable.

My experience with men had not been a Westfield of opportunity. There were no overladen racks from which I could pick this year's best looks, or even last season's clearance offers. There had, in fact, been only a handful of possibilities – and most of those, I had known before I'd even tried them on, were never going to make it to the cash register. Only a couple had shown promise and those I had tried my very best to make fit.

Perhaps, as I made it a policy never to talk to her about boyfriends, my mother imagined that there was a frightening trail of bodies in my wake. Maybe she assumed it was a tendency to licentiousness that made me keep the details of my love life a deadly secret – rather than mundane celibacy and a natural caution about what I shared with my over-invested and less-than-discreet mother. You couldn't play the field when you spent most of the time keeping a low profile and running defence deep in your own half.

You didn't score much if you worried every time the ball came near you.

Only one man had been in my life long enough for aunts, uncles and acquaintances to know his name and ask after him when they saw me. That was several years ago, when my parents still imagined that their older daughter would be the first to get married. Some even knew that he and I were still friends, but only I was aware that he had been invited to the wedding by my sister and politely declined.

There had been no boyfriend since, although I had never considered this a particular worry. Everyone fell in love eventually; my mother's best friend Annie didn't marry until she was in her forties. Meeting a partner was no million-to-one shot. The people who stayed lifelong single were those who chose to or put obstructions in their own path: timid women too scared to socialize with the opposite sex or Brontë-style heroines who turned down love out of mistaken piety, or, perhaps, my cousin Karen.

I belonged to none of these categories. I could be confident that, some time within the next few years, I would once again feel the gut-squeeze of true love. Spending fantastical hours picturing the guy wasn't worth it – why bother, when I knew I'd be getting every detail wrong? All I did allow myself to imagine, occasionally, were those tiny moments when I would glance over to catch my boyfriend-fiancé-spouse looking at me with

near-stupid adoration. For the first couple of years at least.

The conviction that love was all but unavoidable meant I barely gave it a thought at all. Just as I disliked wasting time, I truly hated to waste emotion. There was no point being sad if I didn't have to and so, until he showed up, I was determined not to notice the absence of the man in my life. He certainly wasn't required to bring me bliss; I recognized that today more than ever.

As a person of sudden and extreme enthusiasms, I had experienced plenty of life highs, like the times I was sent to interview my acting heroes and spent the rest of the day quivering with gratification, or the moment that Jonny Wilkinson's drop goal sailed over the crossbar in the Rugby World Cup final. But while those exhilarations resonated somewhere at the top of my emotional range, my current state of delight reached down through my feet and into the ground beneath them. My skin felt warm with love for everyone within those white PVC walls. I'd never imagined that my sister's wedding would be the happiest day of my own life.

When the speeches began, Kate came to sit next to me. It was the first time we had been in each other's company all afternoon and I felt proud of the attention. Our pair of chairs seemed a tiny raft, adrift on the picnic blankets, and we reached out to squeeze each other's hand as our father got up to speak.

Dad began by explaining that Kate had told him to bring it in under eight minutes and on no account to bore everyone with embarrassing stories from her childhood. 'But I've got the microphone now,' he joked, 'so let me tell you a story from Kate's childhood . . .'

It was a sweet story, an old favourite from the parental archive about the tiny girl with the big voice who was the youngest in her class, and had, aged three, been given the starring role in the kindergarten performance at the annual school concert. The class sang 'Ten in the Bed' and she was the little one who had to punctuate each verse with the line 'Roll over, roll over!'

Even at three, her vocal projection would have shamed Ethel Merman and every time she emitted her cry the audience creased up. By the end of the song, the entire hall was helpless. But afterwards, the little girl seemed crestfallen: 'Why was everyone laughing, Daddy?' It had to be gently explained to her that making them laugh was a good thing and that her performance had been a smash hit.

'From that moment on,' said Dad, 'we knew she was destined for the stage.'

The room laughed again now; it was the perfect anecdote for the occasion, endearing, gently comic, infused with paternal pride. The only problem was that it wasn't actually about Kate. The girl in the story was me. The

father of the bride had confused his daughters and spent a good chunk of his speech talking about the wrong one.

I had realized what was happening within a few sentences and known, just as swiftly, that there was nothing I could do to stop it. Turning my head to gauge my sister's reaction, I caught, for a flickering moment, a 'V' of disbelief creasing Kate's forehead. Then she looked back at me and gave a micro-shrug. Our father moved on to another story, one that definitely was about Kate, and finished – a tad over his eight minutes – to warm applause.

Mum appeared beside Kate as soon as Dad was done – 'That silly man! I told him to practise his speech on me!' – and Kate pleaded with her not to make a big deal of it. None of us wanted anyone else to feel bad about what had happened. I, however, felt a hard nub of guilt re-emerge in my stomach. Even unwittingly, it seemed, my childhood ego had crashed the party and disgraced itself. A splinter of shame worked its way under my skin and stuck there.

Marisa had headed home by the time we hit the dancefloor, mugged by the 12-hour time difference; Karen had vanished with the inebriated guest. I discovered I had one more duty to perform as bridesmaid: running interference on the younger kids when Kate and Justin wanted to dance together. There was no separate leave-taking for the bride and groom; we had rooms at the same hotel, since my parents' cottage was already bulging with

guests. It had made me happy, when we booked them, to know that we would all have breakfast together before they left for their honeymoon.

But when we finally reached the hotel the weather was stormy and a noisy wind rattled my window and kept me awake. I lay in bed with an empty feeling, wondering what we would all do next. And when I reached the dining room in the morning, their car was already packed and ready to go. They both wanted to leave in plenty of time to make their flight.

CHAPTER 3

I discovered early in my college days that I had a knack for making friends with guys. This was unexpected as, growing up, I had barely met any. At the all-girls' establishment that educated me, my only encounters with boys were limited to the coaches that took us to and from our respective schools. Those enclosed metal tubes only served to trap and accentuate the most odorous qualities of the postpubescent male. And so I decided to avoid the opposite sex until it developed some manners.

My adolescence was dominated by three obsessions: music, drama and watching sport. Playing the violin disciplined me; acting made me feel alive. Being a sports fan – following cricket, rugby, tennis, motor racing, snooker and anything else I could get a fix of on the terrestrial channels – gave me a sense of belonging. It absorbed me into a tribal identity, one with its own language, rituals and costumes, and one in which my mostly male cohabitants existed at a safe remove, on the other side of a TV screen.

My love of sport separated me, too, from some of the peer pressure at a school where the popular girls were the prettiest ones. There was an unspoken hierarchy of feminine appeal within those brick walls, and all the girls

knew their place in it. I rated myself average rather than ugly but I didn't have the kind of figure or features that were going to slacken jaws at 30 paces. Happily, armchair sports fans had set the bar pretty low when it came to fashion and personal grooming, especially in that pre-Beckham era.

Even a good number of the cricketers and rugby players I admired were surprisingly scrawny or comfortingly tubby, had big ears or squashed noses or monobrows. Looks were far less important than deeds.

And so, for most of my teens, the clothes shopping and make-up application that fascinated my peers had seemed to me a waste of time and effort. When I did finally enter the world of male—female relationships, in the first year of university, I was blind to the concept of sex appeal — unsurprising, since sex itself remained a mystery. What arose to take its place was what I can only describe as 'gameness'.

The cocoon of my single-sex school had squeezed me out with a sexual and emotional maturity several years behind that of my co-ed peers. On the other hand, it had also protected me from some of the worst insults and injuries that horrid boys might otherwise have inflicted on my tender psyche. I emerged from my chrysalis with an optimism and confidence about my place in the world that was, looking back, bizarre in its naivety.

Yes, this suddenly adult world was a steamy and disorienting jungle, filled with exotic creatures whose motivations I didn't understand and whose reactions I could not anticipate. But instead of swamping me in fear, my new environment triggered an inexplicable bravery, which revealed itself in the first week of college when one of the guys suggested playing Frisbee.

For me, sport had always existed purely in the abstract realm. My passion for it had never involved any practical athleticism on my part, had never manifested in lissom physicality or razor-quick reflexes. But I could throw and I could catch, which are the only requirements of Frisbee, a game that is arguably a lot more entertaining when you fail at both. A mixed group of us headed to a nearby piece of parkland and, as the boys spread out across the grass, the girls sat down on a shallow bank to watch.

Why the girls had said yes to Frisbee when they had no intention of playing, I did not yet understand, but the elastic pull of an invisible social cord worked hard to keep me with my kind. I stood uncertainly at the edge of the conversation and wondered whether I'd missed a vital cue. Had the invitation to play been for the men alone? If I tried to join in, would I be ignored or laughed at?

The plastic disc sailed along its polygon course; it moved at speed but none of these guys were exactly ninjas. Besides, I didn't want to sit on the ground watching other

people have fun – *I* wanted to have the fun. I moved towards them and felt the snapped cord fall in my wake.

From then on, when the boys wanted to play Frisbee, or foosball, or French cricket, it was easy to join in, even when the other girls shook their heads and stayed at a safe distance. There was a special camaraderie in this arena of low-stakes competition and, while I might sometimes surprise the guys (and myself), with a tennis-ball hat-trick or a hot streak at the pool table, I quickly learned that it wasn't necessary to be good at stuff to build their trust. It was the taking part that counted.

And so I applied the same principle to much of my social life. I built up my alcoholic tolerance so that I could keep pace with the late-night drinking sessions. If, at the inebriated end of the evening, there was a prank to be pulled or a wall to be climbed, I played my part. I never said no to something because I was worried about looking foolish or unfeminine; it didn't occur to me that I might embarrass or hurt myself.

In fact, I became proud of things I'd never noticed about myself before, like my physical strength or my extremely unfussy appetite (I once won a bet by biting a chunk out of a haddock that was still in its whole, uncooked, seafaring state). When I realized I could withstand very cold water, the challenge to be the first (or only) person to plunge into it became so habitual that I'd do it even if no one was around

to admire my hardiness. This was not always smart and resulted in my closest-to-near-death experience: I once flung myself in a deserted fjord and narrowly avoided an underwater heart attack.

Gameness became my fail-safe way to relate to the opposite sex, and it worked. It also helped me get my first job at a cricket magazine, the only workplace that would pay me to watch all five days of a Test match. I had barely any experience for the role but the editor, a clubbable old gentleman who interviewed me in his favourite wine bar, was impressed by what he called my 'evident chutzpah'.

I was a sportswriter for the next ten years, working in environments and on staffs where I was the only woman. Male friendship became my default. My girlfriends raised their eyebrows when I went out with single guys for evenings I insisted weren't dates – although what really confused them were the holidays. When I announced I was going to South Africa with Richard, or Switzerland with Pete, they assumed I would come back as part of a couple. Instead I came back with an extra three kilos that was all braai and an ankle injury picked up on a black run I really shouldn't have attempted.

Even when guy friends found partners and settled down, our relationships survived on much the same footing. Clearly, if I was mentioned in the marital home at all, I was considered no obvious menace to domesticity.

And so I barrelled happily and perhaps a little obliviously along, celebrating milestones with Pete and Rahul, setting the world to rights with Andrew and Mike, lending a confidential ear to Neil or Richard or Bledi or Rob. I was, all in all, a pretty lucky woman.

Adam was someone I met when I started playing bluegrass music. As if it wasn't enough to work in a male-dominated industry, I had now taken up a completely male-dominated hobby too. I'd been a pretty good violinist in my youth and, after a long pause, I picked up my instrument again, deciding on little more than a whim to throw myself into the country and folk scene. I found a jam in a local bar and my well-drilled classical background enabled me to sit in and keep up with players considerably more accomplished.

Adam, like most of the professional musicians I met, got paid almost nothing for gigging and covered his bills by teaching. It was hard to tell on meeting him whether he enjoyed his career, or the music we were playing, or anything at all. He was one of those guys who looks permanently downbeat, seemingly as a style decision. His small round face was wrapped in beard; the only visible part of him that wasn't defined by hair was the small balding spot at his crown. He and I were roughly the same height and yet gravity appeared to exert a far stronger effect on his frame. His arms hung loosely forward from

the shoulder sockets – perhaps because they had spent most of their lives trained around a double bass – and it gave him the benign look of a Madagascan sloth.

At this stage of my return to music, the nonchalance of the professionals thoroughly intimidated me. Adam was equally adept at bass, guitar, banjo, accordion and all manner of percussion, and he handled every instrument he picked up with a casualness that suggested he was barely aware of his own gifts. The first time I spoke to him, I was so nervous about my own playing that I couldn't stop myself listing every aspect of it I was worried about. He received my tedious ramble in impassive silence. 'Sounds like you need to think less and practise more,' he said, when I finally stopped talking.

Adam never stayed out late drinking, as some of us did. He often left before the jam had finished and I would grumble inwardly because he was usually the best bass player in the room and it was always easier to follow along to his groove than anyone else's. Sometimes he didn't show up for weeks and no one knew why. Even the musicians I assumed to be his close friends – like Andy, who had known him since college and often booked gigs with him – would shrug their shoulders. 'He never tells me anything,' said Andy. 'If I send him a text message, odds are he'll never reply.'

One week when Adam was present, a few of us were

chatting about our weekend plans and I mentioned that I wanted to do a nature walk but wasn't sure where to go. Later – on his way out of the door – Adam told me he planned to drive out to a hiking trail on Saturday and that I was welcome to join him. 'I mean, I do it just for the exercise,' he said, 'so I'm used to going on my own. I might not talk that much.'

It was the kind of invitation you can't help but wonder if you're supposed to politely decline. Still, I generally found company preferable to being alone, however one-sided the conversation might be. So I thanked him for the offer and we made arrangements over email (Andy was right – he really didn't text). On Saturday, Adam picked me up in his car and we headed for some woods on the outskirts of the city.

Despite his hangdog expression and dour warnings, Adam turned out to be easy to talk to, and the fact that he felt no compulsion to entertain or impress was actually an antidote to awkwardness. We spent a perfectly amiable couple of hours roaming along the forested trails, neither of us worried in the slightest whether the other was having a good time.

By the time we were climbing the hill back towards the car park, stepping over fallen branches and kicking cones along the path, Adam was telling me quite unaffectedly about his parents, up in the north. They had divorced

when he was a teenager. His father had married again, to a woman with strong religious beliefs that his dad had since adopted. Trips home were now fraught with silent judgement and a cultural disconnect. 'Dad's who I learned all my music from,' said Adam, 'but now it's like we have less in common than ever.'

I was touched and surprised to hear him share something so personal. Perhaps the open-air environment lent itself to truth-telling, where long pauses in conversation were tacitly acceptable and softened by the background music of tree-rustle and birdsong. Perhaps I presented a different kind of companion to someone with pre-existing expectations of our relationship. There was no sense that I was expected to fulfil the role of helpful advice-giver, or cheerer-upper.

And it went without saying that if I had fancied Adam, or suspected that he fancied me, there would have been a lot more self-conscious second-guessing of what to say and when to say it. Instead, we each walked along with our own thoughts and sometimes they spilled out into the space between us, catching an occasional ripple of recognition or understanding.

I came across a book in a research library once called *The Truth About Man, By A Spinster*. It had been published in 1905 and there was an extremely fey-looking man with a

monocle and white gloves on the cover. I'd picked it up for a bit of a laugh, expecting to find it full of utterly offensive and easily dismissible nonsense. Sometimes it obliged – for instance: 'The woman who makes a friend of a man must first succeed in convincing him that she is capable of following his intellectual flights [snort], then that she is trustworthy [double snort], and finally, for some profound and important reason, cannot or will not marry him.'

But most of it was terrifically astute. The author, it turned out, was a Candace Bushnell for her time; she wrote candidly about her multiple lovers, and the reasons she valued her independence, with a waspish, transgressive wit. She tackled her subjects with a frustrated sigh of experience, from Edwardian society's sexist double standards to men's egregious obsession with sports. She eviscerated men who claimed to want nice gentlewomen for wives but overlooked them entirely to chase younger, far less wholesome creatures.

Some sections made me grunt with recognition and some reverberated with foresight, bravely imagining a day when women would be able to make marriage proposals to men, not to mention steal their jobs. And just as bold a suggestion, in the author's eyes, was the joyful possibility of platonic friendship between men and women – at which, she said 'the writers of our day never lose a chance of jeering'.

She couldn't have known that, a century later, her views would remain on the progressive end of the scale. That the topic of whether men and women can ever be 'just friends' would still be inspiring debate, not to mention one of the greatest romantic comedies of all time. That, two entire decades after Nora Ephron wrote *When Harry Met Sally*, research published in *Scientific American* magazine would claim that men consistently cling to the sexual potential of their apparently platonic relationships. In other words, Harry might be right: the sex part always gets in the way.

When I read my anonymous spinster friend confidently asserting that men and women could, indeed, be friends, I had cheered inwardly. This was what I had always believed, and I knew that my life without its many male friendships would have been much duller and emptier.

After the successful walk in the countryside, I got a four-word text message from Adam: *I liked our hike!*

After this he disappeared for a couple of months, presumably to the touring life that kept him busy but impoverished. The next time I saw him at a jam he was about to take a part-time temp job to help pay the bills in an office not far from my own. We started meeting up for lunch, and the chance to talk about tricky chord progressions or arcane bluegrass recordings in the middle of a stressful work day always made me feel like we were getting away with a petty crime.

These chats taught me a little more about Adam too. I learned that he didn't engage with any form of social media and that you should never try to offer him any kind of recommendation. ('I *hate* it when people tell me I'll like a song or a book or a movie,' he said, with a strength of feeling I hadn't imagined him capable of. 'They're *always* wrong.') I also learned that he would let me know as soon as he was ready to end our interaction. He would finish eating, wipe his mouth with a napkin, check the time on his phone and say he had to leave without a trace of apology, regret or self-consciousness. Neither of us was ever late back to work.

I was still playing at our regular jam most weeks with people who had known Adam far longer than I had. Andy, who liked to describe him as an enigma, was impressed when I successfully arranged for a number of us to go to the cinema together – it had been a long time, he said, since he'd seen Adam show up to anything that didn't involve playing music. It helped, of course, that I hadn't dared to tell Adam that the film had rave reviews.

I enjoyed my new, Eeyorish companion. His deadpan features concealed a bone-dry humour and if you could get him to smile, you felt like you'd won the lottery. It was also a rare treat to know that any invitation that was declined or ignored had absolutely nothing to do with how he felt about you personally. It was such a liberating

sensation it made me bolder; soon I was suggesting outings every week. Adam, in turn, would bamboozle me by suddenly agreeing to come out to a party, albeit one where he would stand in the corner for an hour then disappear in a fog of mystery.

My love for the folk music I was playing had, inevitably, spilled into my work and I'd begun using my newspaper day job as an excuse to write about my favourite artists and travel to gigs whenever I could. There was a particular monthly shindig up north – a variety night with a decades-long reputation – that I was keen to experience and I had already resigned myself to an annoying train journey and a grim overnight in a station hotel when I mentioned it to Adam. He said if I was getting free tickets he would be happy to drive us there and back because it was something he'd always had a hankering to go to.

We met in the afternoon at Adam's place, which was kind of a big deal because as far as I knew absolutely none of his friends, including Andy, had ever seen where he lived. The front door delivered you straight into the ground-floor flat of a shared house with an open living area that appeared outrageously spacious. Then my brain adjusted and I realized it was just empty. There was a sofa, a TV and a small table near the back where the kitchen units were. The only other hint of furnishing came from the various guitars and cases strewn casually across the floor.

There weren't even any pictures on the walls. The unbroken magnolia gave me a flashback to a bedsit I'd known for a couple of months when I first moved to London. At this time, we were all still transitioning between posters salvaged from our student digs and monochrome photos that we would save up our pennies to get framed, so none of us was exactly Peggy Guggenheim. But back then I had managed to date a guy whose unmade room conjured an impression of depressed impermanence that perfectly matched his inner state, down to the microwave, balanced on a stack of DVDs, in which he cooked all his meals.

Adam's similar disregard for anything resembling a creature comfort was unsettling. Who reached their thirties without, you know, *stuff*? What could or should I read into his character from this shambling emptiness? I felt a sudden urge to get going, which was lucky because, as usual, I had cut it fine with the journey planning. It was a two-hour drive to the venue, without accounting for traffic.

As Adam reached for his keys, I all but bolted for the door. He looked at me curiously, then said, in a voice I'd not heard before: 'Do you want to just take a minute?'

'I beg your pardon?' I said.

'You're rushing.' His tone wasn't critical but observational, with a back note of kindness. 'You often rush. It seems to stress you out more. I thought you might like to stop and take a breath.'

I took a breath. He was right; I didn't like pauses or downtime, getting on was how I dealt with discomfort or pain or anxiety. No friend had ever pulled me up on it before. Although to be fair, none of my friends tended to move as slowly as Adam.

The moment gave me a strange glow of satisfaction – the knowledge that he had seen me more deeply than I'd been able to see myself. And, of course, in the event, we arrived at our out-of-the-way destination in plenty of time to have a meal before the gig began. The venue was in an obscure town with few dining options but we found a pub that specialized in burgers and ribs. I chose a combo meal that arrived in a plastic basket overflowing with fries and boned meat and gave up only after my own ribs started to hurt.

The monthly folk night showcased a number of acts and I had contacted the organizer ahead of time to ask if I could chat to them after their sets, looking for fresh angles to write about. It turned out the organizer, Tim, was also the compere, not to mention the town's unofficial mayor. Thrilled that someone from a national newspaper was interested in what they were doing, he had invited us to call on him in the green room at the interval.

The show kicked off with a sister duo who sang songs about heartbreak and looked too young to understand a word of the lyrics. Their voices were passably sweet and

they accompanied themselves on guitars in a manner that suggested they knew most of the chords. I didn't have to look over at Adam to know that he was hating it. I had never heard him say a mean word about another musician but I'd watched him quietly withdraw from enough jam circles to know exactly where his threshold was.

Thankfully, the tween spirits were soon replaced with a bluegrass band that swiftly vindicated our long drive. They were led by a precocious fiddle player whose fingers ran up and down the neck of his instrument so fast they should have had friction burns. At the end of a particularly smoking solo, Adam leaned over. 'If you don't ask him for his number,' he joked, 'I will.'

It was a longish first half and as we got up out of our seats to head backstage, I noticed that the combo meal was working its way to the pointy end of my digestive process. But we had an appointment, plus I didn't want to miss the chance to fawn over the fiddler. Convincing myself that the ominous quiver in my stomach was simply a display of excitement, I worked the packed green room with a tape recorder and a happy smile.

The three-minute bell had already rung by the time I was finished – deftly scooping the fiddler's number along my way – and I realized that Adam had been chatting with Tim throughout the entire interval. It was unusual to see him engaged in small talk and I felt a pang of pride and

gratitude to see him committing to an uncomfortable civility on my behalf. I also felt a pang of something more visceral. Something was squirrelling around in the lower reaches of my gut.

Tim beckoned me to join them and said he had a plan. 'Adam tells me you've written books! We'll get you up on stage to talk about them at the start of the second half. It's not often we have a real-life author in our midst!'

'Thanks, I'd love to,' I said, 'but first I must just . . .' Another bell rang and Tim turned for the door. 'That's our cue!' he said and my legs followed him obediently into the wings even as my brain was screaming at me to make a break for the nearest toilet.

I watched the house lights go down and saw myself walking onto the stage with Tim as if I were having an out-of-body experience. Whether he had meant for me to accompany him straight out there I had no idea, but I knew I didn't have a lot of time to play with. The stage lights were hot on my face and they weren't the only thing making it redden.

Strained, articulated groans were emanating from my middle, and with so many instrument mics on stage I couldn't be sure they weren't being broadcast to the audience. Tim completed his introduction and turned to me with an expectant expression, but I had no idea what he had been saying or what response was required

— all I could concentrate on was the build-up of volatile materials happening inside of me, and their imminently explosive escape.

I gritted my teeth and pushed the facial muscles around them into a clenched smile. 'Thanks Tim,' I said, hoping there had been something in his intro to thank him for. 'Yes, I've written a couple of books and one of them was on music because I used to play classical violin and I came to this kind of music late in my life and I'd heard such great things about this place I just had to come and see it for myself and nowI'mhereI'msogratefulthankyouforhaving-methankyousomuch!' The contents of my stomach made another bolt southward and I waved maniacally at the audience as I backed away from the confused-looking Tim, my mind free-associating the words 'exit' and 'trapdoor'.

In my panic, I fled through a door that led straight back from the side of the stage into the audience. So, having learned my name and occupation, four hundred people watched as I stumbled and shuffled my way to the rear of the auditorium and threw myself against a swing door under a large, well-lit sign marked 'LADIES'. My only hope for the final shredded remnant of my dignity was that the next band started playing before my bowels noisily evacuated. Unfortunately, it takes a really long time to tune a five-string banjo.

When their set did finally begin, I listened to it from my seat in the bathroom stalls. A quarter of an hour passed before I felt well enough to leave, and I hung behind the door, waiting for a loud, upbeat chorus as cover to slink back in. The thought of having to find my way back to my seat, past rows of punters, was mortifying. But I emerged to see Adam standing next to the empty bar, our coats discreetly folded on a stool behind him.

'I wasn't sure if you'd feel up to the rest of the show,' he said, with a matter-of-factness that made me want to hug him. He was also staring at my neck. 'Did you know your skin is all flushed? I think you've had an allergic reaction to something.'

Sure, I thought. Let's go with that.

'So, do you want to stay, or shall we head back?'

This made me even fonder of him.

'I think I'd like to go home please.'

He passed me my coat and steered me gently out.

'Just let me know if you feel ill again, OK?' he said. 'Give me a fighting chance to pull over.'

I still wasn't sure which came first: being a chicken or being a good egg. Did I learn to befriend guys because I didn't believe in my feminine charms? Or was I such a natural at female-to-male friendship that I failed to develop the most basic of flirting techniques?

There was, I suspected, a defensive quality about the persona I presented to the opposite sex. The contents of a man's mind were beyond my understanding, but one thing I believed was that their assessments of women were reflexive and binary: shaggable or unshaggable, hot or not. As an extrovert who craved attention and approval, who feared rejection and loneliness, I was terrified of being written off. The only way to escape the male gaze's potential death-ray, it seemed, was to be off their radar completely. Maybe if I didn't try to impress anyone as a sexual object, I could skip right ahead to being liked and respected.

Perhaps that's why I leaned into the parts of my personality that seemed most palatable to the men I knew, the qualities that were both non-threatening and undemanding. I favoured my chest voice over my head voice and saved my higher vocal range for irony and impressions. I talked about sports, pretended to know about cars, quoted the Monty Python bits that every man my age knew from memory – anything to shortcut me through the dangerous first-impressions stage.

Prioritizing friendship over romance seemed like a mature and mentally healthy way to live, and it rewarded me with a rich roster of relationships. My approach saved me from many a disappointment, I was sure. The older I got, the more prudent it seemed to assume that anyone I met and liked was already spoken for.

But it was also possible that my techniques for making myself sexually innocuous were working *too* well. They were, perhaps, a little self-defeating.

There is a piece of cod-wisdom regularly dispensed to single women: romance will arrive when you least expect it. I had assumed it would make its own travel arrangements, too. After all, there were only really two options. Either a new encounter would spark immediate chemistry or one of my existing friendships would magically blossom into an all-consuming passion.

Was I mentally friend-zoning myself with every man I knew? Favouring certainty over ambiguity, I tended to assume that no guy found me attractive unless and until they chose to make their feelings very clear (by telling me). Perhaps I was damaging my own chances of potential romance. Perhaps my auto-response to men was pre-emptively discounting it.

This was what was in my mind as I watched Adam playing bass for a restaurant band in a slightly bourgeois seaside town. It was September and we had been creeping further and further into each other's lives all summer. The invasion had been discreet and gone unmentioned: after-work drinks, music sessions at people's houses, cinema trips that morphed into late-night pizza. There had been more hikes too and I enjoyed those the most, rambling along side by side with our defences down.

This was when we shared our realest hopes, the ones almost too precious to be admitted out loud. For instance, while Adam was a plenty versatile musician, the style he longed to master was jazz. He would sit at home listening to Nat King Cole records and transcribing the bass parts; he'd stay up late writing his own solos. When he was asked to stand in for a friend at a weekly restaurant gig, performing Rat Pack covers to wealthy diners, he told me, repeatedly, how nervous it made him and how poor a job he was likely to do. That was how I knew he was secretly delighted.

I had told him I wanted to come and watch. 'Not the first one,' he said. 'But maybe if I do it again.' So when he got the call a second time I booked a table and took along my Aunt Jane, who was celebrating her 80th birthday and had a thing for Dean Martin. The band was almost exactly what I had imagined: a keyboardist trapped against the back wall because there was no room for a piano, a trumpeter who muted his instrument so as not to endanger the pace-makered clientele. The singer was more of a showman than a vocalist and he spread his casino-style charm as thick as the cream-of-leek soup.

But my attention was fixed on Adam, who stood at the back of the group beneath a furrow of concentration. Every few bars, he'd hear something he liked and a smile would saunter across his face; in between, it hung around the corner of his eyes. I was well aware of the allure that

can attach itself to any kind of performer in the discharge of their duties. Many are the musicians who become intensely more attractive the moment they pluck their strings or toot their horn. This was different, however. It wasn't seeing Adam's talent that was giving me unexpected feelings – it was seeing him happy.

When he came over to join us at the interval, he couldn't have been more thoughtful to my aunt or keen to make her birthday a good one. He brought her a glass of champagne, asked her what songs she'd like to hear in the second half and promised to get the band to play them. When we slid out after dinner, he gave us a wave from the stage. 'Well, Adam's just a lovely man,' said Jane on the way home, and I didn't disagree with her.

I met up with Andy a week later; he quickly guessed what was on my mind. 'I'll be honest, I assumed you were already dating each other and just not telling anyone,' he said. 'I've never known Adam spend as much time with anyone as he does with you.'

'He's never mentioned any girlfriends,' I said. 'I assume he's had . . . some?' I thought back to his bleak-looking apartment and how few women I knew would have chosen to hang out there.

'He's never talked to me about that stuff either.'

'I just want to know whether saying anything will ruin our friendship.'

'Well, you know him well enough to know he's never going to put himself out there. But he's pretty straightforward and he's a really good guy. If you're honest with him, he'll be honest back.' Andy shrugged. 'What's there to lose?'

Andy's sincerity was comforting. And his words inspired another realization: I wasn't a timorous twenty-something any more, convinced her world would shatter with embarrassment if a guy turned her down. I knew who I was and I liked that person, so if Adam didn't find that person attractive, I would shrug my shoulders and move on. We could still be great friends – I did, after all, excel at that. Besides, there was no *way* I was imagining the chemistry.

It was the first time I had ever told a guy I liked him in written form and I was so proud of my bravery and all-round grown-up-ness that I shared the message I sent to Adam with Marisa, Kate, cousin Karen and Aunt Jane. Then I forced myself to leave my phone in a different room so that I wouldn't spend every sixth minute checking that it was still getting reception.

A couple of hours went by without a reply. My rational brain reminded me that Adam was a deep-thinking introvert who would need extended alone time to process this game-changing message. My gut told me to brace for a rebuff.

It was another two hours before the reply arrived: *Sorry for such a delayed response. I enjoy spending time with you but I'm hesitant because I wouldn't want anything between us to become uncomfortable.*

Well, I thought, there it is. Our friendship is more important. But this is still a win! I have spoken my truth and emerged unbowed; I have broken the vicious circle of male–female relations. I have proven Nora Ephron's Harry wrong.

It was just like my optimistic spinster had insisted in her book. Platonic friendship was, as she put it, 'a very beautiful and inspiring thing' and 'free from the dross of sordid self-interest'. When passion was removed, it allowed men and women the chance of being 'perfectly sane together . . . and of seeing, through each other's eyes, fresh beauties'.

Two weeks later, Adam stopped texting me entirely. We never saw each other again.

CHAPTER 4

Before Mulan came along, it was fashionable to blame Disney and their walk-in closet of princesses for the gender-skewed life expectations of young girls. The first film my parents ever took me to see was *Bambi*, so it is possible that is was there I absorbed the message that my role in life was to be fought over by a pair of stags and give birth to a couple of adorable fawns. But I always preferred Disney's wry ensemble pieces – *The Black Cauldron*, *The Sword in the Stone*, *Robin Hood* – to its classic fairy-tale romances.

And anyway, it would be disingenuous to pin hundreds, even thousands, of years of sexist storytelling on the inventor of Mickey Mouse. Distressed damsels who only find happiness when their prince rides in to rescue them have been filling girls' heads with romantic longing for centuries. Snow White is a 200-year-old German woman; Sleeping Beauty is getting on for 700. Cinderella is probably older than Jesus Christ.

We impart these stories of epic, circumstance-defying romance to children not just before they can read, but years before they'll have any concept of sexual attraction. It's preparation, presumably, for the world of adult relationships and a way to understand the social norms

that children encounter – how humans, like many other animals, live two by two. Even if our own immediate family doesn't contain two parents, those stories introduce us to the mystic union of love as our most fulfilling and pleasurable destiny.

Kids react differently to this discovery. Some reject it out of hand – 'I'm *never* getting married!' – and their parents give an indulgent smile and tell them they'll feel differently when they're older. Others incorporate the new information into their play, using it as structural scaffolding in their innocent fantasies.

When my sister was six, for instance, I married her to one of the little boys who lived next door to us.

She was a shy bride – the wedding was very much my idea – but it was a beautiful ceremony, held under the climbing frame at the back of our garden, a steel chuppah for the occasion. The groom's older brother was his best man and the bride carried a bouquet of dandelions. After the service, which only took three minutes as I couldn't remember all the questions the vicar was supposed to ask, we toasted each other with imaginary glasses of imaginary champagne. I told Kate that I should probably get married to her new brother-in-law, for symmetry's sake.

I was already a devoted bookworm and, as I'd grown, my reading had progressed from the woodland-creature stage (*The Wind in the Willows*, *Winnie-the-Pooh*, *Watership*

Down) to the clever-children-besting-appalling-adults phase (Roald Dahl), before hitting the questing-searching-yearning shelves of the school library. *Twilight* hadn't been written yet, so I probed my prepubescent emotions through the pages of fantasies like *The Dark is Rising* and *The Chronicles of Prydain*. As I fell asleep at night, I liked to weave myself into the stories, bravely throwing myself in harm's way only to require a last-minute rescue by whichever character I was currently infatuated with.

Even though I grew up in a house dominated by busy, competent women – my mother was a lawyer and her mother, who lived with us, kept our home life functioning – there seemed, as I approached teenagehood, to exist a previously unknown state of security that only a male hero could offer. My father was a quiet, practical man who held down the calm centre of a voluble and volatile household and I knew little of the hidden anxieties and sacrifices he faced to keep his family provided for during the recession of the early 1990s. But the male characters in my books – and in the TV shows we watched together – resonated on a different frequency. They promised a happily ever after.

Reading the classics only made it worse. Handing *Jane Eyre* to a relatively literate and unusually suggestible 12-year-old girl is probably as irresponsible as offering

her a drag on your cigarette. The geysers of emotion that went off in me as I encountered Mr Rochester were so overpowering that I was sure they were a bit wrong and ought to be kept secret. I thumbed over my favourite passages so often my copy reached the flimsy, dog-eared state of a comic book – or another, more illicit kind of magazine I'd heard of but never encountered.

The sophistication and elegance conjured by those kinds of 19th-century novels were part of the allure. They were a more enticing vision than the one from my front door: the grey, boxy outline of Luton town centre. But it was their message that really called to me. The charged emotions of romantic destiny reached across the centuries and grabbed me by the ventricles. To love and be loved: this, surely, was what life was *for*.

A host of other imagery was feeding into my neural network to reinforce the idea. Television and film communicated the same thing, though more sexily – be it the broad-shouldered Kevin Costner or Sean Bean and his lopsided smile. The heroines I saw on my screen tended to end the story in the arms of the man who had proven worthy of them.

But it was the literature that had the weight of authority behind it. Things written in books were profound and true because, well, they were written in books, and even more so when they were written by famous authors of

whom your schoolteachers approved. If early feminists like Jane Austen and the Brontë sisters showed me that the greatest joy to be had on this earthly plain was in fighting but ultimately falling in love with your soulmate, who was I to disagree?

And if they told me that a single existence was a lonely, frustrated or bitter one, there wasn't much in the modern culture around me to refute that. The unattached characters in my favourite TV shows and movies were continually on the hunt for romance, be they Friends looking for their lobsters or Bridget Jones staring down the barrel of a tub of Häagen-Dazs. Even the defiantly independent Carrie Bradshaw spent most of her energy sieving the city for true love.

Marriage was a well-respected institution in our household. My parents had never shown any inclination to leave each other, even if their own relationship seemed far less interesting or passionate than the ones I read about. Divorces were fairly rare among both my friends' parents and my parents' friends. They were also treated with a very middle-class reserve, meaning they were never discussed around me and my sister, even, or especially, when they occurred within our own wider family.

I was probably a traditionalist before I could pronounce the word. A successful life meant following convention: getting a good job, getting married and living in a

sequence of houses that you upgraded over time. I plotted my future accordingly.

My plan was to marry at 26 – which was, frankly, daringly late. Since my parents had met at university and regaled me with stories of their many friends who had done the same, I assumed that was where my grand romance would begin. By my calculations, a wedding in my mid-to-late twenties gave me a generous grace period to make sure he was the right one.

I factored in at least a couple of minor yet dramatic break ups, which would only enhance our great love for each other, and plenty of time to establish a career. A one- or two-year engagement was a given and I'd left myself an ample buffer to bear two children before turning 30 (since being a 30-year-old mother was still, in those days, considered outré). And then I actually went to college and learned my first great lesson in being unable to bend destiny to my will.

I did not meet my life partner. I did fall painfully and messily in love for the first time, mining all the depths of drama I'd missed out on as a primly chaste teenager. It was the kind of affair you wouldn't have believed if you'd watched it in a soap opera: there were noisy scenes where I yelled, poignant scenes where I cried and clichéd scenes when I sat prodding at a plate of food, unable to get down a mouthful. This was sexual attraction

approached with the same over-confidence and under-experience as student cooking – bubbling over, boiling dry and leaving the bottom of the pan in an unsalvageable state.

After graduating, I gained a little more experience, dating what recipe books might describe as a 'small handful' of men, although never for more than a couple of months apiece. I was both dumper and dumpee, and the guys themselves were different enough in character and background to make me feel that it was all useful calibration in my pursuit of The One. But my ambition to be married at 26 soon fell away and by the time I actually turned 26, I had forgotten it entirely.

And yet, that year did turn out to be the most romantic of my life.

My friend Pete was living in a house of four guys, two of them a couple. The other, called Matt, was single and Pete often talked about him with an affection that was only partly exaggerated for my benefit. It worked, too – whenever Pete took a call from this mystery guy and I was in earshot, I was deeply curious to know what they were discussing. Sometimes Pete even dropped my name into the conversation – 'Oh, I'm just with Emma . . . yeah, she's well . . . OK – Emma, Matt says hi' – as if I were already acquainted with the anonymous rumble on the other end of the line.

It was obvious that we were being set up and when the invitation came – to a house party that the four lads were throwing for no reason in particular – I was excited by the prospect. I had even spoken to Matt on the phone by this point, thrown on there by Pete in a moment of mischief – 'Here, you can say hello to her yourself!' I'd been intrigued by the low voice, which sounded curious but not unconfident and left silences I gabbled into a little too eagerly.

The party was a disappointment. Well, not the party itself, which was thick with people and barbecued food and noisy enthusiasm, and proved just how popular the boys were. I had been promised that Matt was tall – around six-foot-two, Pete had said – and he lived up to his billing, although he bent forward as he talked and wore a shirt and a jumper that hung off him as if he were trying to hide something under them. But I barely got to speak to him; he kept quietly disappearing into other rooms and conversations, and I spent the night getting drunk with Pete's gay housemates, both of them high-spirited and much more my speed.

With a little encouragement from the boys, I missed the last tube and stayed over, Pete magnanimously giving up his bed and sleeping on his own floor. The next morning I woke to pastries and takeaway coffee, which they had already been out to gather. Matt was working on

a crossword and I sat next to him in one of Pete's T-shirts, puzzling it through, the three of us settling into an enjoyable camaraderie. There seemed to be a permanent suppressed smile stored in a twitch at the side of Matt's lips, as if the world were a source of endless wry amusement. He was an extremely soothing presence and I liked the sensation of sitting next to him several times more than was normal.

It was Pete's idea to ask Matt if he wanted to have brunch, which was, according to an Australian like Pete, the perfect daytime date. I'd texted Matt a little after the party, leaving agonizing lacunae between each message so as not to seem too keen. Whether Pete or I bothered to pretend that he was going to join us at brunch I can't remember, but either way he found himself emphatically busy that morning. So Matt and I ate eggs Benedict at a café near my home, which turned into a long walk along the canal that ran behind it, which turned into drinks and an early supper at a waterside pub.

By the time he walked me back to my front door, it was almost sunset. I lingered on the step, meaningfully. He leaned in towards me.

As soon as he was out of earshot, I phoned Pete in an outrage.

'He gave me a *hug*, Pete. A hug! Then he turned and walked away. I thought you said he was *interested*!'

Pete was apologetic. 'Wow, I don't know what to say. I thought he was.' He paused, guiltily. 'He can be a bit hard to read.'

It wasn't for several more months that I learned the truth. Pete was returning home to Australia and I went to his house for the emotional farewell, helping him pack his gear into a taxi and waving him goodbye. Later that day, I got a text from Matt asking if I wanted to have dinner.

It turned out that he had felt some anxiety at the thought of complicating his and Pete's mate-ship by dating a mutual friend. With Pete safely on an aeroplane, we went out for pizza and ended the night in his bed.

Almost immediately, something about him felt different to the guys I had dated before. The others had enjoyed arguing as a primary pastime – nothing serious, just playing devil's advocate in the face of my over-certainty on topics like politics, religion, sport and any form of western culture on which I considered myself an expert. Matt, however, seemed happy to listen to what I said without the need to correct me. If he disagreed, he changed the subject or waited till I'd talked myself out of breath. This was both infuriating and alluring because I never knew exactly what he was thinking.

On one early date, by the time I reached the climax of a long barrage of opinions, Matt had retreated into such a monkish silence I was sure he must be angry about

something I'd said. Annoyed that he was withholding and secretly worried that he was judging me, I prodded and harangued him until he finally spoke again. 'I'm just a bit overwhelmed,' he said. 'You've told me a lot of different things and I don't know how I'm supposed to feel about any of them. So I don't think I have anything to respond with just now.'

No one had ever challenged me like that before. I'd thought of introversion as a weakness and shyness as a social flaw, but Matt owned them without embarrassment. Too many people and too much chatter left him feeling swamped and a bit lost so he avoided social situations with more than eight people and when his housemates did force him into a party, he found ways to retreat and escape.

And yet he was always ready to make an effort and a good impression with my friends. When I introduced him at my birthday dinner, his self-effacing manners and reassuring baritone delighted the girls, who were convinced he reminded them of someone. Ally stared at him dreamily all night, until she squeaked, 'I've got it! He's Colin Firth!' and then badgered him until he finally agreed to deliver her favourite line from *Bridget Jones's Diary*. 'I like you just as you are,' he told her, and she almost swooned into her chocolate pudding.

It didn't take long to realize how lucky I was. My boyfriend was selfless and thoughtful, and left me in

no doubt of how much he cared. He accompanied me to exhibitions and plays and movies in which he had only the slightest interest. He made secret bookings at restaurants that I'd read about in magazines and bought surprise tickets to see my favourite band play an outdoor gig at Hampton Court Palace. And even though he hated shopping, he let me take him to department stores where he bought better-fitting clothes and smarter shoes and the eau de cologne I liked, until the bank froze his card and phoned him up to report unusual activity.

He was also a clandestine romantic. For the next couple of years, I was indulged with cheap-flight weekends to Dublin, Rome and Barcelona, and whisked to Paris by Eurostar. We dressed up nice and ate out at fancy places, and everyone knew my boyfriend was smart and gracious and loved me a lot. Matt wasn't a demonstrative guy, yet when we walked down the street he always reached for my hand, quietly sliding my cuff up my arm a little, so that no part of our palms wasn't touching.

I only remember him delivering a single cross word in all the time we went out. I had been frustrated with his navigating as we drove through a foreign town and sulked my way through lunch, until eventually he looked at me with a cool stare and asked, 'Do you *want* to have an argument?' I blanched at this unprecedented show of steel and mumbled into my pasta: 'No thank you.'

In our second year together, I committed an act of financial self-sabotage: I left a happy, stable work situation to try new things as a freelancer. It was a bold move for someone whose emotions already oscillated in a wide range; now they reached new extremities, between the euphoria of possibility and the crashing fear of failing to cover my next rent. Matt, now living in a flat only a short walk from mine, was a perfect shock absorber, regulating my moods with his calm, forgiving presence, indulging my self-absorption only so far and no further.

We were settling into the kinds of behaviour I associated with long-term couples – cooking dinners with M&S ingredients, going to the pub down the road to watch sport. I enjoyed playing at being a grown up while suspecting that I didn't have to be one for real because Matt was doing the job for both of us. The fact that I rarely paid enough attention to detail to book myself onto the right train or that my absent-mindedness with diaries often resulted in embarrassing triple-bookings was now mitigated by an observant partner who kept catching my mistakes before I made them. It had never been easier to be me.

Our friends and family thought we were made for each other. So did Matt, who made casual yet undemanding references to our future. It seemed all but inevitable that one day he would ask me to marry him, when our frothy

young love had thickened into the kind that bound us together like treacle. He made me feel safer and more stable; I encouraged him to be bolder and step out of his comfort zone. Even our worst traits seemed to make the other one laugh.

Case in point: Matt loved long walks. It was one of his favourite activities, and something that always sounded fun to me in theory. As we donned our coats and wellies, I'd be keyed up with the spirit of adventure. Two minutes after we started hoicking through the damp grass I would exaggeratedly complain that I was tired already. Matt seemed to derive a certain private entertainment out of my childish posturing and once I had made him laugh, I cheered up and behaved myself. His patient good humour and wide range of long-suffering expressions were the perfect counterpoint to my exhibitionism.

Pete had been urging us to visit him in Australia and we arranged a long holiday, devising an itinerary that would take us up the coast from New South Wales to Queensland. My job situation was causing me ongoing anxiety, even though I was finding work, and I was acting unusually crabby around poor Matt. So I threw myself into planning our grand road trip – it felt like a welcome distraction from the future as much as from the present.

We spent the night before we were due to fly at my place. Matt noticed that I was in a particularly irritable mood.

'Have I done something wrong?'

'No!'

'Are you nervous about Australia?'

'No.'

'Is it about what you'll do when we get back?'

'Yes. Probably. I don't know.'

'You know you don't even need to think about work for a couple of weeks. You won't have time to worry, we'll be having so much fun.'

'It's not that.'

'Then what is it?'

I couldn't stop myself; tears and words bubbled simultaneously, as much of a surprise to me as they were to the man next to me.

'I'm worried that I'm not in love any more.'

I hadn't realized it myself until I said it out loud. Whatever I'd been feeling I had hidden behind the knots in my shoulders and my permanently tensed jaw. Now the source of the strange and unwarranted irritation I felt around my boyfriend suddenly lay exposed between us and I wanted more than anything to swallow it up, to never have said it at all.

My timing was horrible. Expensive, non-refundable flights and hotels had been booked. Our friend was expecting us. There was no question of changing our plans. A decent person would have managed to suppress

their feelings for at least a week or two, out of guilt or compassion or pragmatism; I was incapable of making it through the evening.

I stared at the ceiling. Matt was silent. He asked me why I thought that and I told him I just wasn't feeling any of the things I thought I was supposed to feel as his girlfriend and he said that he was very sad to hear it. Then he subsumed his own emotions with a nobility that would have shamed most of the Round Table. We would go to Australia as friends, he said, and we wouldn't worry about any of this until we came back home. His kindness made my lack of feelings seem even more despicable. I sobbed into a pair of my dirty socks because there were no tissues to hand, and even if there had been, I didn't deserve them.

An extended holiday in a land of blue skies and white sand did not clarify anything – in fact, it did the opposite. Travelling was exciting, Australia was intoxicating and Matt was my perfect travel companion. The idea of not being in love with him made no sense at all. If our trip proved anything, it was that I didn't like Matt any less: the more time we spent with each other, the more I appreciated what a special person he was. We had the easiest and most comforting of companionships and I didn't remotely want to give it up.

And so I convinced myself that the warm feelings I had towards him were a sort of love, and he seemed to have

enough conviction for both of us. I appeased my conscience by telling myself that I'd been honest with him about my doubts. After that, it was horribly easy to return home with a semi-casual relationship that both of us wanted in our different ways. And I got to enjoy the familiarity of being a girlfriend without the commitment of one.

I was very aware that I was becoming the villain in my own story. Matt was on hand to accommodate me and my capricious affections, and I revelled in his attention and drew on his calm stability, which seemed to anchor me in a way that nothing else could. I still knew, deep down, that I couldn't stand up in a church and promise myself to him for the long haul.

There followed a series of break ups that did me no credit whatsoever. Ignoring all best practice for these things, we hovered around each other, hanging out as friends, enjoying an occasional illicit kiss. I understood that I should be keeping my distance, getting out of the way so he could he happy with someone else, and I was ashamed of my selfishness. But I didn't want to lose my best friend.

It took a long time before we managed to free ourselves from each other's orbit. No one who knew us could understand why it hadn't worked out; some even tried to encourage a reunion. It didn't help that whenever I talked about Matt it was impossible to conceal how important he

was to me, how I marvelled at his brains, his tenderness, his decency.

My female friends were sorry for me in a way I couldn't be for myself. I hated that I was being offered sympathy for breaking someone else's heart – it felt wrong. They even tried to comfort me by telling me that I had 'done the right thing', which made me writhe with shame, since I had repeatedly done anything but. Still, they didn't know that because I'd never brought myself to confess the whole truth to anyone.

'You can't force yourself to be in love with someone you're not in love with,' said Kate, to whom I'd admitted more of the details than anyone else.

'But I want to be,' I said.

'Well, we can't have everything we want. Matt isn't the guy and that's sad for both of you. But now it's over, you'll each move on and meet the person who *is* right for you. This is a good thing – think of all the people who get married to the wrong person and regret it later.'

I couldn't think of it – I just couldn't imagine it. Why would you marry someone you weren't head over heels for? I understood that economic reasons had forced people to do it in the past but Jane Austen and Charlotte Brontë had taught me that it ended in misery.

Kate was right about Matt, though. He fell in love with someone else and married them, and I knew he

would make the kindest, most generous husband in the world. I, meanwhile, came out of the relationship with my romantic notions as fortified as ever. They hadn't just escaped unscathed – they'd been positively reinforced. Whatever invisible, indescribable element was missing from my feelings towards Matt, whatever fairy dust turned a best friendship into lasting passion, it was clearly beyond manufacture.

And I was prepared to wait for it.

CHAPTER 5

The pub at the end of my road was, unapologetically, a sports bar. But it was a comfortable rather than sticky one, with large leather sofas and a giant projector screen they pulled down from the ceiling at the weekends. I'd grown attached to it because of its really crispy chips and its readiness to open at 8am when there was an important cricket or rugby or tennis match happening on the other side of the world.

I sat at one of its larger tables, waiting for my friends to arrive. It was a relatively busy evening and every so often someone would come over to ask if they could take one of the chairs, and I'd have to say that I was really sorry but I'd actually reserved them. Then they'd look pointedly around my empty corner of the room and stalk away with a filthy look.

Nothing could muddle my emotions like a birthday. The urge to celebrate – or more accurately, to be celebrated – was irresistible. I had no problem being the centre of attention; for me, the greatest danger of throwing a party was the threat of disappointment.

Every invitation contained the possible sting of rejection, like a swarm of self-addressed wasps. No matter how many people said they were definitely going to show

up and did, it was the apologies that landed harder. When I saw a text message that began 'Hey hon! I'm so sorry but...' I would often stop reading and put my phone away until I knew I had the fortitude to read the rest.

This inspired no little resentment towards all those friends whose birthday celebrations were arranged for them by their partners. Parties just seemed so much classier when you didn't have to do the organizing yourself, when your husband sent out an email saying, 'Hi everyone, Bryony's too modest to tell you this but it's been a really big year for her – she's been made partner, not to mention running her first Ironman *while* pregnant with our beautiful twins! We're so proud of her and we'd really love you to come and show her how much she means to us all!'

Those birthday girls didn't have to spend a week locked in negotiations to pin down a date when more than two of her friends were free, only later discovering that it clashed with a tube strike or a royal wedding. I envied surprise parties the most – the incumbent arriving to an instant shower of presents and affection. No amount of hinting had ever resulted in me being thrown one.

Anyway, this birthday was exciting because I'd managed to wrangle my university friends and the whole gang were coming – even Hywel, who had gone to Taiwan to train as a plastic surgeon then moved back to Wales, from where it was hard to winkle him. I couldn't wait;

there was a part of me that only seemed to come alive in their company. It was a distinctively juvenile part, admittedly; a part that revelled in Hywel's smutty jokes and Tom's purposely outrageous behaviour, a part that would describe itself as private just so it could force a joke about private parts.

I knew some people who didn't like mixing their friendship groups – they found it awkward, they said, they didn't like having to introduce people and host them and make sure they got on. My college mates were, however, excellent minglers. I was excited for Marisa and my other London friends to meet them; sometimes I worried that people I had got to know in the years since university were meeting a vanilla version of me, someone who wasn't quite living up to her promise. With the gang, I knew who I was – an entertainer, an extrovert, a big fish in a small pond. In their presence, I felt invincible.

Marisa, true friend that she was, showed up early to help me defend my corner table and the rest weren't far behind. The uni gang presented me with a joint gift – a casserole dish from Habitat that would supposedly last the rest of my natural life and a photo album of our greatest hits: Tom dressed as a Spice Girl; Laura and I in nun habits; Ben in a tux, bow tie undone in a manner he hoped to suggest either George Clooney or Roger Moore, it wasn't clear which. I emitted small shrieks as I flicked through them.

My other guests indulged me as I narrated the hilarious things we'd done together, as if no one else's uni life had been as blessedly crazy as mine. I was the birthday girl, after all.

Someone pointed to a picture of Hywel standing in a forest, his boxers tucked up cosily around his genitals.

'What's going on there, then?'

'Oh God, *that* night . . .'

'I've never been so scared in my life.'

'Which one of us was driving?'

'It was Tom, surely.'

'No way, it was me! *I* had to do it!'

We retreated into our shared memories, talking over each other until the story found its way out of its own accord. We had been on holiday, driving across America in the summer after graduation. Everything had gone wrong from the moment we bought a car and it broke down at the first motorway toll we stopped at. It had needed towing again in the middle of West Virginia, where we spent the night camped in a quasi-hurricane and one of our tents slid away down the hill.

On the particular occasion of this photograph, we had driven late into the night through some darkly wooded national park – we couldn't afford campsites with amenities, not once we'd blown our budget fixing the car. It was getting on for an hour since we had last seen

a streetlight and when we stopped at a railway crossing with its barriers down we finally realized how closely our evening was beginning to resemble the end of the first act of an Appalachian slasher movie.

We had sat nervously in the car and locked the doors, listening for an apparently non-existent train, working ourselves into a greater state of terror with every additional minute. Eventually, hyped with fear, we decided we would rather risk the collision than spend one more moment idly waiting for hillbillies to carjack and murder us. Whoever was driving – me? Hywel? – had slammed their foot down and zigzagged us through the gate at top speed as we screamed for our lives.

When we finally made it to our remote camping spot, there was no sign of another human being. But there was a battered old caravan, empty. Whether its occupants had already been slaughtered or whether it was the part-time abattoir of a serial killer currently watching us from behind a tree we were undecided, but it was agreed that we would forgo our policy of separate girls' and boys' tents and all huddle together in co-ed fright. Nobody slept a wink and by the time the sun came up we were hysterical with relief that we'd survived the night. Oh, and Hywel had tucked his boxers round his balls.

If you had asked me back then, that summer that we drove across the States, I could have told you that the next ten years of my life were going to revolve around these half-dozen people. We had come together in our first year and spent most of our second and third in each other's rooms, in various states of wild excitement and sleepy inebriation. We talked and drank and drank and talked until we fell asleep on chairs and rugs and dusty floors because no one wanted to be the first to leave. There was nothing we couldn't have told you about each other, from the precise nature and location of our most embarrassing medical conditions to the names of early childhood friends we'd never even met.

These people were infinitely more important to me than my further education and as intrinsic to my sense of self as my own bones. I couldn't imagine anyone knowing me better or bringing me more happiness. There was no question that our postgraduate lives would be entwined. There was, however, a geography issue. Tom, Laura and Hywel were all medical students, heading to another university town to complete their training. Ben, Jon, Ally and I, arts graduates without portfolio, moved to London in the hope it might contain some sort of work we were equipped to do.

My naïve forays into big city life were exhilarating but every time we visited the other three at their shared house

I was overcome with jealousy. Here, among a clique of fellow medics, our friends were continuing the life we'd had together. In a living room filled with cheap brown furniture that had come with the house, I watched our private running gags superseded by hospital in-jokes and banter based around infectious diseases. The faux-adult dinner parties we held – since none of us had the funds to go out to restaurants – only emphasized our difference. We were the guests, they – and their new friends – were the hosts.

Something else was changing too. At college, a cesspool of gossip and shared bodily fluids, it was impossible to enjoy a cheeky snog without everyone else knowing about it before you'd woken up the next morning, usually with a corresponding hangover. Now my friends were dating people I hadn't met or vetted. Ben, who I shared my first flat with, talked to a cute guy at a party and disappeared for 72 hours; by the time I saw him again, he and his new boyfriend John were as easy in each other's company as if they had recently celebrated a landmark anniversary on a Mediterranean cruise. The fact that John was mild-mannered and self-effacing did not alter the fact that I considered him a dangerous outsider and secretly hoped that he was a passing fad.

The medics, confined to their alternative reality of student debt and endless exam revision, didn't get much

time away from the training hospital. Tom and Laura were diligent and brainy in a way I admired without seeking to emulate. As undergrads, they had managed to combine hedonistic high jinks with early morning lectures and an obsessive absorption of the curriculum that landed them both with first-class degrees. Med school, they insisted, was harder and Laura reassured me, during long phone calls, that they weren't having fun without me. 'Honestly, we don't have time for parties,' she promised, in the soothing maternal tones that had seen me through many a post-adolescent meltdown. 'You're having a way funner time than we are.'

On one of these calls, Laura told me she had been out with a guy called Mark, a fellow postgrad who, having spotted her walking through a park, had quite literally pursued her to ask her out. She didn't fancy him but she'd been so caught off guard that she said yes anyway. Then he had turned up for their first date with a bunch of flowers.

'It's a bit much,' she said, her voice tinged with embarrassment.

'Oh, it's kind of sweet,' I replied. 'Did he pay for dinner as well?'

'I couldn't let him. He's doing a teaching diploma.'

'Is he at least good looking?'

'He's all right. He's not *bad* looking.'

'Well, keep it up until you run out of vases.'

'We'll see.'

Laura had always been the most sensible of our friends. She had inherited her mother's profound practicality and patience from her father, a vicar, along with the odd eccentricity – such as the fact that she couldn't remember her left from her right. This seemed a terrifying trait in a soon-to-be doctor but was apparently acceptable in the world of medicine as long as she didn't want to be a surgeon.

From the moment she materialized in my life – unpacking boxes in the dorm room next to mine – Laura and I had been paddling our way to independence together. Our shared canoe saw us through waters infested by second- and third-year sharks; we kept each other afloat as we rode the exhilarating rapids of all-night drinking. We had only ever fallen out once, early on, when I'd staggered into her room after a particularly debauched evening, wanting to tell her all about it, and found a guy I'd been seeing asleep in her bed.

It was her honesty and calm that had saved our friendship then, not any magnanimous display of empathy or forgiveness on my part. How Laura never lost her temper with me, however, was a mystery. I was a noisy, messy and frankly unhygienic housemate – she would hunt for the week-old, furred-over cereal bowls I had forgotten under my bed when the smell became unbearable – and my exuberance of emotions regularly demanded centre

stage at the expense of everyone else. Somehow, Laura was content to be my earthing rod.

When we moved to separate cities, I relied on her to help me bear the new demands of being a young twenty-something. Looking for a job. Struggling at the job I got. Suddenly finding the job too easy and wanting to move on already. I called her when everything felt so hard I didn't think I could make it and I called her when everything was going so well that I couldn't believe it. Laura let me talk and talk until I'd worn myself out, listening with genuine concern. After maybe half an hour, towards the end of our conversation, I would finally remember to ask her how she was doing. She was always fine, stoically bearing the same worries as me with a far less dramatic approach.

Laura deserved an award in her role as Best Supporting Friend. That's certainly how I saw her at the time; maybe that's why I assumed that her own love story would feature me in a major role, or at least require my input and approval as a test audience. Instead, Laura's relationship proceeded so quietly and modestly that I honestly forgot it existed half the time. Mark was the subplot everyone forgot in the edit.

When Laura came to London, she barely mentioned her boyfriend; when I visited her, she was careful not to invite him to the activities we had planned together. 'Acting couple-y' – planning everything with your other half, using the pronouns *we* and *our* – was still categorized as a

major crime among our friends and those who committed it were mocked in their absence and stripped of whatever respect we'd had for them. I'm sure I met Mark somewhere along the line – probably at some come-one-come-all picnic – but the encounter left no lasting impression.

To celebrate the end of their training, the half-dozen medics who Laura and Tom hung out with organized a trip to the south of France. When they told me I was invited too, I was flattered. Clearly, this demonstrated not just how important I was to my friends but also how well I had fitted in with their new set. Those extraneous people I'd made so little effort to get to know must have thought I was innately cool.

When Laura told me Mark was coming too, I felt a little cross. Mark was not cool. If he was cool, I'd have paid him more attention. 'I'm so glad you're coming,' said Laura. 'It'll be great for Mark to have someone to talk to who isn't a boring medic.' So now it was even worse: I was a confirmed add-on. The rest of the gang would be making each other laugh with sperm-based humour and I'd be stuck discussing lesson plans with Mark.

However, I wasn't planning to turn down a week on the Mediterranean coast. Travels with my friends during the summer holidays had been some of our most formative experiences but they had also been gruelling. On our American road trip we'd been too poor to afford motels

and eaten nachos for breakfast. A two-month backpacking tour of India had left us all with flea bites and amoebic dysentery.

The medics, though, confident in their future income, had rented a comfortable villa in the countryside outside Nice, surrounded by lavender and sunflower fields. It had a small pool that we clinked around in like ice cubes in a G&T and a rustic kitchen where the men flexed their egos in endless rounds of competitive cooking. Their fancy creations were accompanied with the rosé from nearby vineyards, which we bought by the gallon in plastic containers – pink as nail varnish and the most delicious thing to ever have passed our lips.

I had never felt more grown-up.

Sure, the guys still liked to brag about the most disgusting things they'd seen on their ward rounds and they couldn't resist the urge to pull each other's fingers. But that was the price you paid to be friends with the opposite sex. This far from the hospital, moreover, the medical chat was at a minimum – there were always more immediate matters to discuss, like how great French butter was, whose turn it was to drive to the Carrefour and whether we would ever actually be bothered to go out sightseeing.

In this atmosphere of lazy luxury, I glimpsed a desirable future. Surely it would make sense for me to fall

in love with one of these doctors-to-be, becoming a fully accredited member of their clique and guaranteeing myself a lifetime of enviable vacations. Most of the guys were still single. They were smart and funny. If one was rather shorter than me, and another attempting to disguise a prematurely receding hairline, these physical traits would only become endearing once the oxytocin started flowing.

And there was one guy there who seemed to be making a special effort to seek me out. Unfortunately it was Mark and he was really cramping my style. I'd be sitting in the courtyard, trying to shower the company with witty observations, and he'd dowse the sparks with his infuriatingly prosaic responses. At mealtimes, he would make a point of sitting next to me and ask me earnest questions that drew us out of the general conversation and into a side discussion on hiking equipment or theology. I answered automatically, while listening to the hilarity at the other end of the table and seething with resentment.

Everyone seemed to get on fine with Mark, which I couldn't understand because he did not fit the template that Laura and Tom and the rest of my little gang had established for our friendship. For a start, he never talked pretentiously about books, films, music or art – he just didn't to seem have strong opinions about that stuff, which I took to mean that he was unsophisticated. He didn't speak like us either. There were no quick and

casually cruel put-downs in his conversation. He did not load his utterances with irony so heavy you could house radioactive waste in it.

To me, this all indicated a lack of spark. It didn't seem possible that Laura could feel that strongly about him. Throughout the holiday, we never saw them holding each other's hand, or snuggled on a sofa, or leaping away from an illicit clinch when we walked in on the pair of them alone. Having previously spared Laura's relationship no thought at all, I was now convinced that it was a dud.

On our penultimate evening, Laura and I stayed out late on the loungers by the pool. The only lighting came from beneath the water, where an underwater bulb transmitted an eerie iridescence, and the enfolding darkness encouraged a confessional atmosphere. We'd both been reading novels – mine a short, modern portrait of sexual obsession, hers a long, multi-generational narrative of a family through time. I was soon holding forth about the electric, ecstatic passions I considered myself an expert on since my turbulent college romance.

'I don't know,' said Laura. 'It all sounds rather exhausting to me.'

'But it's the greatest feeling life affords!'

'I was there. Most of the time you were just very unhappy.'

'I wasn't!'

'We remember it differently.'

I sniffed, haughtily. 'Well, I can't understand people who settle.'

'I think everyone settles,' said Laura. 'They just settle for different things, in different ways. Not everything has to be fireworks.'

Her measured wisdom nettled me.

'Are you settling, then?'

Laura sighed. 'You've been a bit rough on Mark this week.'

'I've tried my best. I just don't think he's good enough for you.'

'Well, thank you for your concern but it's not about what you think, is it? You're not the one who has to be in love with him.'

I goggled. '*Are* you in love with him?'

'Yes, I am. It's happened quite gradually as I've got to know him but I think I always knew that's how it would be for me.'

I scoffed. 'So, what, if he asked you to marry him, you would?'

'Yes.' She paused. 'And I think he probably will ask me, at some point soon.'

I felt suspended in shock, like a reckless driver who insists on taking an upcoming corner at speed then finds themselves rolled in an inevitable ditch and dangling

upside down by their seatbelt. I was simultaneously chastened and annoyed.

We were silent a while; I could think of nothing more to say. Laura walked to the house and I stayed outside, allowing an air of tragedy to settle upon me. I moped on the lounger as the temperature grew cooler, determined that someone should notice my absence. Eventually one of the young future-physicians succumbed to curiosity and came out to join me.

He was, I realized now, the handsomest of the bunch. I heaved a few sad sighs in his direction and confined myself to enigmatic remarks about a 'difficult' chat I'd just been having. There was twinkly starlight and a scent of lavender and it seemed only natural that he should lean over to comfort me, and that the comforting should lead to a kiss, which it did.

For some reason – let's blame all those female novelists – I was convinced that aloofness was sexy. Plus, I was still cross with Laura and I didn't want her to think I was over our quarrel. This was clearly the chapter where the downcast heroine rebuffs her suitor's advances, piquing his ardour and strengthening his resolve. And so I broke off the kiss, murmured something heavy with poignancy and walked back to the house with a troubled step.

The handsome doctor never tried it on again.

Laura and Mark were engaged within a few months. I was asked to be a bridesmaid, which was highly effective in forcing me to drop my reservations and get behind my best friend's relationship. After all, these things were beginning to get serious all around. Tom and Jon were both going out with women they didn't try to play down as casual flings. John, meanwhile, was a regular visitor to our flat; he spent most of his time in Ben's room, materializing occasionally in the corridor like a semi-mythical creature.

Ben and I, the most determined to fend off the boring conventions and distractions of adulthood, acted as the social secretaries of our friendship group. We were adamant that the special bond we all shared should not be allowed to atrophy or dissolve. And so it was that we came up with the Leave Your Partners At Home weekend, which was every bit as militant and discriminatory as it sounds.

The inaugural event took place in the early days of both Laura's and Ben's courtships, when Mark and John were all but invisible to the rest of us. It was supposed to be a mini-break of sorts but since none of us had any money, we crashed at Tom's parents' house, just outside the M25, and bunked on air mattresses in their attic.

We did the full circuit of our respective parents' homes over the next couple of years. Our cloying respectfulness in the presence of the grown ups and our humble eagerness

to do the washing up would dissolve into utter disregard as we stayed up all night screaming with laughter and drinking their spirit cupboards dry. In the daytime, we went for hungover walks just as far as the next pub, where we soused ourselves in chips, gravy and beer.

The weekends achieved their purpose perfectly, establishing a pattern of behavioural relapses that allowed us to believe that nothing was really changing. We stayed hooked on each other. We talked about all the things we wanted to see and do and promised to do them together, planning dream trips to all parts of the world, getting an advance high from the fun we would have. Perhaps I struggled to be interested in my friends' girlfriends and boyfriends because it seemed impossible that anyone else could make them feel as deliriously happy as we did.

It didn't bother me that I was always the one who coordinated diaries, who nudged and nurdled our get-togethers into existence. In fact, it was only natural; I was the chattiest of us, the most inclined to spend long hours on the phone, acting as the information hub that connected our disparate locations. My friends loved each other but weren't always great at dropping one another a line. A call from me conveying the news that Hywel was a bit poorly or Ally had just got a promotion was often the prompt they needed to reach out.

But everyone was busy and transforming a nebulous

enthusiasm into a solid commitment was tougher than it should have been. I sensed danger down the track, like an old man in a Western with his ear pressed to the rail, hearing the approach of a train bringing carriages of troublesome newcomers.

Laura and Mark's engagement was the ball bearing that falls at the start of a Rube Goldberg machine, its smooth and inconsequential motion triggering an ever-proliferating complexity. The medics were on rotation now, consigned to a tangle of neon-lit corridors and nightshifts, in towns and cities they never had time to see. Mark, meanwhile, had taken a teaching job at a school in an entirely different part of the country.

The next time I broached the idea of a Leave Your Partners at Home weekend, Laura explained she wouldn't be able to come. 'Emma, weekends are the *only* time I get to see Mark. I'm not going to tell him I can't see him because I'm off visiting other people.' I relayed the news to Ben, hoping for some sympathy. He replied that the idea had always had a limited shelf life and to be honest, John was getting miffed that he wasn't invited either.

So we attempted to rebrand it the Bring Your Partners Along weekend. This didn't have the same ring and entailed twice the diary work but it did force us to give our poor parents a break and actually rent some accommodation. We gathered in a featureless village in the Midlands because

it was equidistant from our various locations, started drinking on arrival and didn't stop for 48 hours.

And, of course, it was so much fun that I regretted I'd ever been resistant to the concept. The presence of Hywel's and Tom's girlfriends curtailed their scatological side, making them the most pleasantly behaved I'd ever witnessed. Jon's girlfriend brought an organizational verve that got us out of the house and Mark's map-reading skills saved us from getting lost on our rambles. Ally and I, with no partners of our own, shared a twin room and whispered, as we fell asleep, how surprised we were to be enjoying ourselves. When it was time to leave, everyone said we must do it again soon.

The logistics never allowed for it. We were, in the few years that followed, buried in an avalanche of weddings. Not just the weddings of the principles – Laura first, then Tom, Hywel and Jon – but of seemingly everyone we knew and everyone they knew too. Schoolfriends, work friends, partners' friends . . . summers suddenly became scheduled around these nuptials as if we were minor royals doing the Season. And each brought its own satellite events: the engagement parties, the hen and stag dos, the baby showers that swiftly followed. For a short while, it seemed as if the bulk of my social life was spent celebrating people's relationship status updates.

The mass plunge into matrimony clogged my calendar

and made me a little envious – mostly of the attention and the chance to pool funds and live in a bigger house, not to mention the opportunity to have the contents of your kitchen updated for free. But I didn't covet anyone else's romance. No one's passion seemed quite as grand as the one I had pictured for myself and other people's choice of partners continued to baffle me. I remained confident that when my Prince Charming arrived, I would trump everything that had come before with the greatest love story of all time.

Meanwhile, I could approach everyone else's Big Day as a sampler for my own. There was no time to indulge in self-pity when you were silently sizing up the colour of the bridesmaids' dresses or making a mental note of the table settings. I developed surprisingly strong opinions on floral arrangements and a rule about the maximum tolerable time lag between confetti and canapés. If more than 20 minutes elapsed before I was able to pop a salmon blini in my mouth, the wedding received an instant black mark.

I was, at this stage, increasingly tortured by the notion of being in my late twenties and the existential threat that posed. I had spent much of my twenties worrying about how old I was getting, each year seeming to pass without quite enough to show for it. Every step closer to 30 felt like a stage curtain slowly falling on the most important and exciting years I would ever have.

And it seemed increasingly like I was being robbed of something. There were many fun things I still wanted to do with my uni friends, most of which had been put off because of the hecticness of wedding planning. But the Great Settling Down didn't seem to settle things at all.

I read in women's magazines how friends tended to 'go dark' for six months after their weddings and a girl just had to wait until the couple emerged from their love cocoon, finally bored of each other and ready to re-engage with their wider relationships.

That wasn't my experience. When I called Laura a few days after she returned from her honeymoon, to ask about Mauritius and check that Mark was still the man of her dreams – he was – she told me I must come round and see the new house.

'Yes please! Can I come for the weekend?'

'Of course! We've got my parents coming this weekend, then we're off to see Mark's parents the following Saturday ...'

'What about the one after that?'

I heard her flick the page on a wall calendar. 'We've promised to have his best man Dave and his wife over. Sorry, this sucks ... and we're away again the week after. Can you wait a couple of months? I'll check that Mark hasn't organized anything else without telling me ...'

This new cycle of marital commitments was relentless and endemic. Phone calls plugged the gap but my tribe seemed to be vanishing around me, retreating into the woods with their superior survival skills and leaving me to fend for myself.

A more rational being would have calmly accepted that their friends, now operating as a part of a unit, had effectively doubled their social engagements and halved their free time. I saw it as evidence that I wasn't as important to other people as I had thought. I was slipping down the friendship pecking order, usurped by couples who offered twice the entertainment value and knew how to talk about house prices.

When Bring Your Partners Along did eventually get a reboot, a weekend was impossible, so we shaved it down to an afternoon. Two of the group had children already and some of the partners were too busy to come. We met at Hyde Park and walked through Kensington Gardens, where Tom's toddler took tentative steps beside the memorial fountain and we watched on, wondering how much damage the sharp concrete edges might do to a soft skull. When we talked about our jobs, I realized how little I knew about what everyone was up to.

They had come to my birthday party, though. Here they all were, dressed up nice just to see me, making admiring

nods at the sports bar, which I was showing off as proudly as if it had been my own home. And it was a joy to pinball between them, to nestle alongside as one after another they draped an arm over me with a casual air that said: she belongs to us.

I introduced them around, hoping to bask in the liquid glow of validation that comes from hearing your friends discuss how they know you, and share notes on your delightful qualities. Instead, they were soon recounting my most embarrassing moments. 'I was just telling your mate Rahul about your twenty-first,' said Tom. 'Remember how we got you a massager from the Body Shop, but wrapped it up to look like a vibrator, and made you open it in front of your parents? You went *so* red...'

'Oh, anything can make her blush.'

'She's blushing now!'

'Has she told you about the time she knocked Jon out cold with a squash racket?'

'No, but I want to hear it ...'

I cringed a little and opened a gift from Marisa – a resistance band and a spiky massage ball. 'They'll be really good with your pilates exercises,' she said.

'You're doing *pilates* now?' Hywel yelped with mirth. 'That is hilarious. I didn't know this. Did we know this?'

Jon shrugged. 'I didn't know it.'

'I have a bad back,' I said, diffidently.

'Pilates is really good for your back,' said Laura.

'It is,' I said, suddenly reluctant to talk any more about it.

'No, I mean, good for you, pilates.' Hywel was still giggling. 'You'll be telling us next you're teetotal.'

I bristled inwardly. It occurred to me that while my friends were quick to recognize the outward symbols of adulthood in each other, to me they attributed an enduring irresponsibility. Hywel gave me a hug and told me he loved teasing me, which was almost an apology. 'Isn't it great how we can always just pick up where we left off?' he said.

'It is great,' I replied, even though I knew we weren't making new memories, just reconstituting old ones.

Laura and Tom were the first to leave, checking the train times and racing to relieve their babysitters. 'Sorry to be so boring,' they said, as if in response to some unspoken reproach. I wished I could prove to them that my life was moving on too, just not in ways I could point to, or dress up in Mini Boden.

CHAPTER 6

Rose was the oldest person in the room. She was also the gobbiest. She looked as brittle as a pink wafer biscuit and every time we levered her out of her chair and onto her walking frame, I was sure I was going to accidentally snap the arm I was responsible for. But she ruled over our weekly musicmaking like a cockney von Karajan. ''Ere she is,' she announced when I arrived. 'Everyone shut your traps and get out your songbooks.'

It was a testament to the newspaper where I was now working that they encouraged me to lead a sing-song at a nearby daycare centre for the over-70s and turned a blind eye to my overlong lunch hour every Friday. What it was that Rose and her pals found so enjoyable about my ham-fisted renditions of old music hall numbers bashed out on an ill-tuned piano, I could never fathom. But they were regularly delighted at my arrival and joined in with gusto, including several for whom English was a second language.

Once everyone had worn out their voices, rolling out the barrel and giving Gracie Fields a few free underground spins, they liked to keep me there under the pretext of a cuppa and a custard cream, grilling me about my personal life.

'What are you doing this weekend?' Rose would ask

and I would fill her in on the upcoming events – a day trip to the coast, perhaps, or an afternoon at the cinema, or drinks and dinner with friends. She was always impressed by how full my diary was. Whenever Patrick, a former army sergeant and the only man in the room brave enough to interrupt her, asked if I had a feller yet, she would yell back at him: 'Give over! She's still only a baby!'

Rose spoke with the authority of a 95-year-old single woman; she had outlived her husband by more than a decade. 'You enjoy yourself while you can,' she would tell me, almost every time we saw each other. 'You'll be a long time married, take it from me.'

Her advice was in marked contrast to my mother's, who was, as I drifted through my fourth decade, increasingly anxious about my failure to find a partner. When things had failed to work out with Matt, there had been a few delicate references to the fact that she would love me no matter what and whoever I wanted to bring home would be fine with her. Once I'd explained that I wasn't actually gay, I sensed a loss of sympathy and a growing frustration that I just wasn't trying.

'It's not that I don't think you're very capable,' my mother said, 'but the truth is, life is just easier when there are two of you to help each other out. You still have the same struggles but it helps to bear the load when there's someone to share them with.'

I nodded diplomatically and told her I believed her. And it was true, there were plenty of things I had to handle alone that I wished I could find someone to give me a hand with. I got grumpy lugging shopping across London on the tube. I didn't enjoy cooking, especially for one. It wouldn't hurt if there was someone nearer than half a mile away who I knew well enough to help me when I was hopping around my bedroom half-clothed, struggling to do up a particularly tricky zip at the back of my dress.

It would also have been nice if just once someone else could have stayed home to let in the boiler repair man and pretend to understand what he was saying. If there was one thing I hated, it was being solely responsible whenever something went wrong in my flat. Still, I was getting bolder with my have-a-go DIY efforts. Dad was always on the other end of the phone to advise how to unblock a sink or change a dimmer switch. When I made a mess of a wall in my over-ambitious attempt to put up shelves, I just covered it up with a couple of posters. And, of course, there was no guarantee that my eventual boyfriend would be any more practical than me. If the earnestly bespectacled intellectuals who populated my social sphere were any indication, then he absolutely wouldn't.

The truth was that I was a fairly privileged woman with a decent job and a home my parents had helped me to buy just before the financial crash made getting a mortgage

all but impossible for people on single incomes. The convenience of urban life and modern technology, not to mention the invention of Uber, meant that I encountered few scenarios requiring a male helpmeet or chaperone. My house was so close to a station that I could hear the groan of the brakes as the trains passed my garden and I was never afraid to walk home alone down my well-lit street, however late the hour.

If anything, the peel-off of the people I'd been closest to, as they moved in with partners and out of my ambit, had made it feel far more valuable to cultivate friends than to waste evenings chasing after men I might have no lasting interest in. 'And anyway,' I reasoned, 'the more friends I make, the more likely that one of them's my future husband.' Even my lawyer-mother couldn't argue with that logic.

I was pretty pleased with how well my plan was working. I had got to know my neighbours – both the young couple renting the flat beneath mine and the older, long-term residents in the houses either side. George, the retired bouncer and Essex hard man who lived in the basement flat to my right, was particularly sociable; we spent so much time in each other's gardens that when a part of the brick wall separating them began to crumble we replaced it with a gate.

George had become an expert groundskeeper during

a long stay at Her Majesty's pleasure and he was generous with gardening advice and plant cuttings. In return, I would bring a bottle of wine and sit on his well-kept patio, trying not to look too horrified at his stories of smuggling contraband past international customs. He was another person with complete confidence in my marital prospects. 'Lovely girl like you, you'll be fighting them off,' he used to say with an avuncular wink, and even though I shrugged modestly, inside I was silently agreeing: I *was* a catch, wasn't I?

All in all, I thought I was getting just about as much out of life as an independent woman could hope to, with the exception of regular sex. And to be honest, when I fell into bed each night, exhausted from a busy schedule of work and socializing, I wasn't convinced I'd have had the energy for it.

My mother, however, remained unconvinced that my life was a complete or completely happy one. This was obvious from the way her ears pricked up every time I mentioned a man's name in passing: 'And is this Neil . . . nice?' she would say, employing the kind of spycraft you learn from watching *'Allo 'Allo*. If I objected, she got defensive – 'I'm just asking if he's a *nice person*! No need to bite my head off!' – and in the end, I started leaving the male cast members out of my stories, just to make it easier.

A few times she tried to set me up with her legal protégés; I gave in once, just to satisfy her. Unfortunately, she had not sent adequate instructions to the young solicitor in question. He had no clue as to my mother's brief or strategy and decided to bring along his cousin. I spent a very dull evening as a listening post while they discussed what their various family members were up to these days.

Still, it wasn't as misguided as the time she and I went to a West End musical and she noticed the man next to her had come to the show alone. Immediately befriending him with the sheer force of her personality – my mother was very charming – she then demanded I swap seats with her, loudly disclosing her bladder control issues as an excuse.

I knew he was gay, he knew he was gay and, to be honest, most of the patrons sitting nearby and watching this desperate display of mother love knew he was gay. At the end of the show we exchanged phone numbers anyway – it is always nice to discover a new theatre-going companion – and we met up a few weeks later to watch the guy he was crushing on in an amateur production of *Oklahoma*.

I knew that my mother's efforts, and her underlying concern, came from a place of love, not to mention an era of more traditional gender roles. But the more she told me I should be thinking about the future, the less I wanted

to consider it at all. Abandoning the mental comfort of a contented present to dwell on an anxious future I couldn't control seemed like madness. Better not to look too closely, I felt.

And anyway, wasn't she a feminist too? Hadn't she broken through the glass ceiling, the first one of her family to earn a degree, the first woman to make partner in her law firm? Hadn't she sent me to a school whose motto was 'Independent Girls, Independent Women'? So what exactly did she think she'd been preparing me for, if not a world in which I could get by just fine on my own?

We never talked about it, except for once. It was during another trip to the theatre – I'd interviewed a director and when he invited me to see his new comedy, I took Mum as my plus-one. I suspected she would like the show, but I *knew* how much she liked the idea that I was operating in rarefied cultural circles, where comped tickets came with a couple of drinks vouchers for the bar.

The show was warm and funny and we loved it; we fell out of the lobby and onto the street like giggling drunks and made a spontaneous decision to get takeaway burgers from one of the chain restaurants nearby. She squeezed my arm as we stood waiting by the counter. 'Dad and I are *so* proud of you, you know,' she said, 'living in the big city, doing all the things you do.' She sighed. 'If we could *just* find you a husband.'

I attempted to stifle an electric surge of annoyance with a laugh, and what I thought would sound like a lighthearted rebuff.

'Yes, sure, let's focus on the one thing I haven't managed to achieve.'

'Don't get cross with me,' said my mother.

'I'm not cross, I just don't know why you're saying I need a husband immediately after you've said I'm doing great.'

'Because we worry! We won't be around forever. We just want to know there's someone who'll look after you when we're gone!'

'Well, I'm sorry you're worried but you telling me that doesn't help. It just makes *me* worry.'

Without a sound, my mother turned and walked out of the door. I waited awkwardly for our burgers, the soles of my feet prickling with embarrassment. When I got outside, she was standing by the edge of the kerb.

'What was that about?' I asked. 'Are you actually angry with me?'

'Oh, I can't do anything right, can I? I tell you that I want you to be happy and I get shouted at.'

'I did not shout at you. I just told you the truth.'

'Well clearly I'm a terrible mother. I don't want to talk about it any more.'

We walked back to the car in uneasy silence, the

courgette fries seeming to weigh particularly heavy in their paper bag, until I caved.

'I'm sorry, Mum. I do want to meet someone but I can't magically make it happen. It's not in my control.'

Arguably, there *was* a way to magically make it happen, at least according to the adverts on the tube. And I'd already given it a go, a good go, in fact – my mother just didn't know that.

It was in the late noughties. The analogue methods of securing a boyfriend – getting purposefully drunk around a guy you liked, kissing him, then doing that a few more times until you were a couple – were finally catching up with the advent of online shopping. Internet dating had arrived.

Prior to this, courting someone on the internet was seen as something done by loser guys who couldn't rely on their natural charms and dodgy guys who probably had a secret family or a connection to a cult. If you did end up with someone you met online, you made sure you had a cover story that could fool MI6. The first time I went to the wedding of a couple who found each other online, their origin story was never referred to once, and even though we all knew, it was considered incredibly insensitive to bring it up.

But now the question wasn't whether you should look for love on the web but where. Suddenly, my laptop

seemed full of possibilities. A burgeoning industry was touting for my custom with month-long free trials and I was a perfect target: 25–34, female and highly suggestible. (A beautician once convinced me that skincare regimes only worked if you used them in conjunction with other products from the same brand and I kept slavishly to this rule for years before Ben told me that I was an advertiser's wet dream.)

For several months, I surfed the introductory offers, fascinated by the differing demographics of the various sites. Would I fall for some wealthy banker or trust-funded cabinet-maker on My Single Friend, which seemed to source its public-school clientele exclusively from Fulham and Chelsea? Might I settle down with a suburban accountant and his pre-existing border terrier courtesy of match.com? Or was I going to spend my weekends at the Southbank, discussing Christopher Nolan's early films with the gentle north London intellectuals I'd met on Guardian Soulmates?

We had not yet entered the easy age of swipe right. Before Tinder, online dating required a considerable time investment, one of the many hidden costs of searching for love. Simply setting up a profile was a tortuous exercise and for all my innate confidence, I was not suited to self-marketing. It was hard to put into words what, if anything, made me uniquely appealing to the opposite sex.

(Everyone, it transpired, liked 'going out', 'trying new things' and 'chilling out on the sofa with a DVD and a glass of wine'.)

At the same time, my pride chafed a little at putting myself out to tender and I became rather more interested in weeding out time-wasters than making myself approachable.

'Are you sure you want to describe yourself as "independent" three separate times?' said my sister, when I asked her to look over what I'd written. 'I mean, bravo for showing your feminist side but you're giving the impression you don't actually want a guy at all.'

'Fine, I'll only say it once. Anything else?'

'I'm not sure that loving cheese and the novels of Anthony Trollope are especially sexy qualities.'

'I thought they were adorable quirks.'

'They make you sound like a smelly old woman.'

'I'll take them out.'

'Yes. And lose the bit in "what I'm looking for in a man" where you say "someone who can spell".'

If there's a more passion-killing experience than sitting at a laptop, typing up your application for the job of girlfriend until you have a headache from the screenglare, I've yet to encounter it. It does, however, wear down your resistance. As soon as I got my first expression of interest from a guy, I agreed to a date with

him immediately, out of relief, exhaustion and gratitude at his pioneering spirit.

He was a mathematician who wore Oxfords and to whom I felt no attraction at all; he took me to a Japanese restaurant 'hardly anyone' knew about, that served 'real' sushi, just like the stuff he'd eaten when he'd lived there for a couple of months in his gap year. He asked me how many CDs I owned, a weird question I realized he'd only asked so that he could tell me that he had three thousand. By the end of the evening, I was just happy it was over. Then, as we parted ways, he said, 'This was nice, maybe we could do it again?' and I nodded automatically out of politeness and kicked myself all the way home.

For some reason, I felt honour-bound to see the second date through; it is possible that this established the unnecessarily masochistic pattern into which my internet dating career then fell. I went on many second dates with people I wasn't interested in, my theory being that if a man was prepared to ask me out a second time he had earned the courtesy. And anyway, the few guys I had fallen for in the past were rarely ones I fancied on first sight. The chances that I would recognize a potential lifelong attraction over the course of a couple of gin and tonics and a packet of salt and vinegar crisps seemed slim.

My calendar quickly began to fill with social engagements that I was barely looking forward to.

Meeting and getting on with strangers were things I generally enjoyed – it was part of the attraction of my work as a journalist – and I liked to feel I'd been a decent date, regardless of the outcome. But second dates were often far less entertaining than first ones. The anything-was-possible-and-who-knows-he-might-actually-look-like-Jude-Law frisson of anticipation had gone. I was now required to ask intelligent questions about his career/community work/*Call of Duty* addiction and at least appear to be interested in the replies.

I couldn't shake the feeling that I was somehow doing internet dating wrong. It just seemed to require so much *effort*. Initially, I pored over profiles with the heightened concentration of a kid surveying pic 'n' mix shelves while fingering the fiver in their pocket. But I quickly learned to make snap judgements and to cut and paste my replies. Even then, maintaining a presence on these sites required at least half an hour of correspondence and admin a day, from basic vetting to low-key flirtation and advanced diary management. I devoted a lot of time chatting to strangers I never even bothered to meet up with. After all the legwork it was often a relief to go on a date – to turn up at a bar, have a drink and talk about my day with someone who was duty bound to smile.

When I came across Philip's profile, he sounded smart and funny, and as if his DVD collection would cross-

match with mine by at least 80 per cent. The more we messaged, the more we noticed we had in common. We did the same job, in the same industry; we had a shared love of supposedly boring sports like cricket and snooker; we liked the same obscure folk music; we both considered ourselves awesome at pub quizzes. (Who knows, these may also have been the reasons we were still single.)

When we did meet up, after a week or two of online chat, the similarities got freakier. It turned out we lived just round the corner from each other; we were regulars at the same bars and had a couple of mutual friends. It was almost a miracle that we had never met before.

The date went smoothly – our experiences were so similar in every regard that any conversation topic raised was a good one. We had arranged to go for a drink and then to the cinema – I chose the film, he pre-booked it – and during the screening he whispered in my ear just enough to make me feel important without being an unwelcome distraction from the plot. On the way home, I sent a text to thank him and got one straight back, proposing a second date at a restaurant I'd wanted to try for ages.

It was as if he was the male version of me, so I was a little disappointed that I didn't find him sexier (after all, that didn't reflect well on me, his female doppelganger). But he was good company, so we went out again, and then again. On our fourth date, we met up for a picnic by the

river and when we had eaten and drunk and packed things back into bags, we began to walk towards the train station. I never saw him reach for my hand – I just felt something close in around it quite quickly and forcefully, and it was only then that he murmured a quiet, 'I might just hold your hand if that's OK . . .'

I said no. Actually, I didn't say it so much as shriek it. At the same time, in an instinctive bodily reaction, I tried to wrest my hand back. He had gone for the interlocking-fingers option from which there was no quick release. So there we were on what he evidently thought was a romantic walk, while I stood stock still, squawking and wrenching my arm away. I offered an immediate apology but it was never going to be enough to rescue either of our dignities. We both left mortified and never communicated again.

It was possible, I realized, that I wasn't made for this game. I knew plenty of people for whom internet dating had been very successful – immediately so in the case of my friend Rachael, who fell in love with and ultimately married the first woman she'd gone for a drink with. Others told me that you had to commit to the process, that if you wanted to get something out of it, you had to invest time in it the way you would in any hobby. But this wasn't fun like a hobby. It was more like taking on a second job to pay the bills.

My biggest issue with online romance was that I just couldn't find the romance in it: every endeavour felt transactional and loaded with judgement, every interaction potent with an agenda. Some sites made me feel positively bad about myself. I knew that I was going to struggle to find dates on My Single Friend when I was pretty much the only user whose profile photo wasn't taken on the riviera or the ski slope. I had to stop using the one faith-based site I tried when I kept getting creepy messages from men 20 years older than me.

But really, it was eHarmony that broke me.

I had begun with great hopes for a site that connected lonely hearts using psychometric testing and an algorithm that rated their compatibility based on their mostly deeply held values. The claim was that this laid the foundation for a healthy, lifelong relationship – eHarmony wasn't just finding you a date, it was offering you the person even your conscious mind didn't know it was looking for. Here, I thought, was the magical fairy dust I needed.

The home page looked no different from any other site I'd tried – a little cheesier, perhaps. There was a photo of a gleaming couple, accompanied by the statistic that eHarmony was responsible for 263 people marrying every single day. This sounded extraordinarily hopeful, even if I couldn't help noticing that 263 was an odd number.

The sign-up process revealed that the company took a

rather matronly approach towards its subscribers. Where most of the dating sites I had visited encouraged flirting through instant chat and email, eHarmony liked to act as a chaperone, keeping a keen eye and a restraining arm on you and your prospective lover. Once I had found a likely looking man, I would have to send him an eHarmony-approved 'icebreaker'. Only then would I be allowed to graduate to 'guided communication', which involved choosing five questions for him from a pre-ordained list. He, in turn, would reply from a set of multiple-choice answers. Independent thought was clearly not encouraged.

For a matchmaking site that was supposed to be tailoring its results to my personality, eHarmony sure didn't want me to express any. It was a slight turn-off to imagine that the first thing I might say to my future husband would be 'Wink!' or, 'You seem interesting. Why don't you finish your "About Me" questions?' But eHarmony's promise of a scientifically calibrated questionnaire and the 'psychometric report' it would generate lured me on. I was a sucker for a personality test.

And so I waded into the questions that would tell eHarmony all it needed to know about me to deliver my perfect match. They went on for pages and pages and took me multiple sittings to complete. It was at this stage the process started to feel less magical and more like a corporate retreat for middle managers at a medium-sized

insurance company. At one point I was asked to select my three best 'life skills' from a list that included 'achieving personal goals', 'maintaining an organized life' and 'using humour to make friends laugh'. I felt the charisma leaching from my body; by the time I'd finished, I wasn't sure even I'd date me.

As it turned out, this wasn't a problem. There was a moment of suspense as the screen buffered and the site crunched my data, running its binary judgement over me. Then eHarmony's algorithm delivered its ultimate verdict. 'We're sorry,' read the message, 'we have no appropriate matches for you at this time.'

Computer says no, thanks. It was about as humiliating as being picked last in PE class but without the teacher's compassionate hand on my shoulder, telling me that maybe swimming would be my thing. I checked back in every day for a week and when I still hadn't received a single match, I took a long hard look at the results of my psychometric report. Under the 'Agreeableness' heading, it said: 'You are best described as: Consistently Taking Care of Yourself'. Now I knew why I didn't have a date: eHarmony thought I was a self-obsessed sociopath.

I could have let an algorithm get me down. But maybe that psychometric software understood more than I realized because I knew only one way to react to this: I took care of myself. The very pride that had originally told

me that I didn't need the internet to find me a boyfriend flooded to my rescue. I stared at my computer with the cold, dead contempt of Coriolanus as he addressed the Roman crowd gathered to witness his exile: *I* banish *you*.

Goodbye to those hours of online small talk, to the travel to awkward-to-get-to places at the wrong end of the District line, to the evenings spent telling someone where you worked and how many siblings you had. Adieu to the unnecessary expenditure of emotional energy wondering whether you might ever want to sleep with this guy you just met. I would waste no longer on this bootless pursuit.

There was no need for desperation. I was an inwardly and outwardly attractive woman who was worthy of love and likely to find it in the same haphazard way that had worked for billions of people for millennia. Rose was sure. George was convinced. If I ever wobbled or wavered, I only had to tell my sister in order to receive an immediate string of encouraging texts. Romance wasn't a myth but it wasn't a chore either and, one day, it would come for me.

CHAPTER 7

It was the middle of January. My parents had escaped the bleakest of the British months by flying to Australia to visit some relatives. They had left me with the keys to their small and awkwardly shaped cottage, and I had taken the opportunity to stage a weekend in the countryside for some friends, despite the fact there weren't remotely enough beds for us. Even in my late thirties I had apparently not grown out of slumber parties.

It began with a mishap. While most of us had travelled down together, our mate Chris had made his own way by train and his phone had run out of battery on the journey. While we were wondering where he'd got to, he was wandering around Milton Keynes looking for somewhere to charge it so that he could work out where he was supposed to be heading. When he eventually unplugged an innocent vending machine and resuscitated his Samsung, he discovered that he'd taken the wrong train and that the rest of us were in a different county.

The next day it rained so heavily that we had to abandon our plan for a crisp country walk and were forced to retreat to the village's sole indoor attraction, an ancient yet extensive collection of taxidermied animals. Since we were also missing out on the pub lunch we had promised

ourselves, I ordered a takeaway curry for dinner and tried
to inject some sophistication by serving it by candlelight.
My parents kept a few safety candles under the sink;
I wedged them into metal eggcups to serve as holders and
placed them artfully around the living room. By the end
of the night they had left perfectly singed circles under
everything they had touched.

This was not the first time I'd left my mark on my
parents' home – or their cars, or other assorted items of
value. It was part of family lore that I was the clumsy one.
I never *felt* especially blundering and I still tried to resist
the label, but my legend was inescapable and grew with
every item I dropped or toe I stubbed. It was agreed upon
by every member of my family that I suffered a chronic
lack of common sense. This incurable condition fuelled a
combination of cack-handedness and ineptitude, and led
to widespread outbreaks of mess.

I was the the breaker of wine glasses, the scratcher
of hub caps, the dropper of coffee grounds; I was the
person who never stacked the dishwasher properly or
remembered the items I'd been asked to bring with me,
and who ate the food in the fridge that was supposed to
be saved for a different night. So this latest incident with
the candles was not going to help my cause. I dreaded,
already, the dramatic groan my mother would give when
she was told of it and the queasy sensation I'd experience of

living down to her expectations – of knowing that, in my parents' eyes, I was still not a proper grown up and never likely to be.

My sister, usually prepared to offer a modicum of moral support in these cases, had come to the house the next morning to survey the damage and see what could be fixed before I had to own up to it. My own response to the oncoming trauma was to blot it out with breakfast cocktails. When Kate arrived, it was to a house enveloped in a fug of post-jalfrezi body odour, with top-notes of orange juice and prosecco.

'Want a mimosa?'

She shook her head and waited till everyone was occupied with bacon and eggs then beckoned me quietly upstairs. We picked our way over the sleeping bags and up to our parents' bedroom. Kate's face was so serious I thought she must be mad with me. My brain guiltily scanned the past 24 hours to check if I'd done anything else wrong, beside the candles.

The curtains were still pulled and we stood in the gloom of an underpowered low-energy lightbulb. 'Don't make a scene,' she said, as if she were about to pull a gun on me. 'I'm not supposed to tell you this yet but I'm pregnant.'

My sister had only begun trying for a baby a few months ago, having been ready for one pretty much the moment she clapped eyes on Justin. In my attempt to

convey excitement without raising my voice, I overcooked my facial reaction: a jaw muscle pinged and I worried I'd strained my eyeballs. Kate, however, seemed determined to stay sombre. It was far too early to celebrate, she said, and we had to keep it a deadly secret from our parents. She looked like someone delivering bad news while fighting an inappropriate urge to giggle.

My own reaction was the reverse. At surface level, I was thrilled that the sister I loved had got what she wanted. My happiness for her wasn't a pretence. But it also wasn't the whole story. Even as my slightly tipsy ears absorbed the information that our family was about to expand again, a sober corner of my mind was worriedly picking it apart.

The truth was, I had never enjoyed other people's children. Kate knew this. It wasn't something I was good at hiding, and even hiding it felt like an imposition. But I did understand that indifference to, boredom with and occasional outright revulsion at somebody else's bundle of joy were not socially acceptable responses. As a woman, I was expected to find divine delight in the children I encountered (unless they demonstrated particularly noxious behaviour, which apparently entitled me to judge both them and their parents). The sight of a big-eyed baby was supposed to warm my heart and flutter my uterus. And if a gif of a two year old with porridge smeared across its face didn't melt me, did I even have a soul?

I didn't want people to think I was a psychopath. So I calibrated my reactions accordingly, exactly like a psychopath.

There was an array of stock phrases I turned to when people started talking about their children, most of them gleaned from things I'd overheard others say in similar situations. 'What a cutie,' I said, when shown a picture of a snot-nosed troll staring into a phone camera with a malevolent expression. 'That's adorable,' I breathed, at the story of a peacocking little know-it-all correcting their teacher's pronunciation of bruschetta.

My favourite was, 'Oh, bless,' which was not only utterly meaningless and thus universally applicable but also forced your lips into something that passed for a smile. It had become my go-to at social gatherings in my late twenties, when babies were still a rare commodity among my friends and non-mothers queued up to hold them, passing them hip to hip like koalas at an illegal petting zoo.

None of this is to say that I didn't expect, at some stage, to have one or more myself. 'It's different when they're your own,' I was told, by just about every parent I'd ever met. Children had always been presented as an inevitable part of pre-packaged adult life. So, for a considerable time, they remained on my long-term agenda, in the same way that an electric screwdriver sat on my Amazon wishlist –

a household item I ought to own at some stage, but that felt boring to spend money on right now.

It wasn't that I *didn't* want them – I just, you know, didn't *want* them. 'You'll want them when you meet the right person,' my mother always told me. I was happy to leave it at that and didn't interrogate her hypothesis any further. One grand quest at a time was enough.

As for the fact that I found children mildly irritating – I assumed this was because most children *were* mildly irritating. Why everyone had to pretend to be wryly amused by everything they did eluded me. Wailed demands for more tomato ketchup did not make eating out a more entertaining experience. Siblings competitively naming everything they saw from the train window did not make everyone else's journey pass faster. A changing room full of knee-high hazards did not enhance a trip to the swimming pool, especially if one of them was loudly asking their mummy why that lady's bottom was so much bigger than hers.

I didn't *choose* to be this grumpy around children. When an old schoolmate became the first of my friends to become a mother and I was invited round to see the baby as if it were a new exhibit at the Tate, I felt very conscious of the honour. I bought a tiny item of clothing that cost as much as something ten times its size and showed up to what was billed as Christmas drinks with the family. My

schoolfriend's parents and siblings were there too, people whose company I had always enjoyed.

And yet the moment I showed up, I realized that something had changed, and not for the better. We sat on a circle of chairs eating cake while everyone's eyes remained glued to the baby bouncer in the centre. The place was zombified; no one was capable of carrying out ordinary conversation. This mute, immobile being was sucking the atmosphere out of the room, making everyone around it as uninteresting as itself. I felt like a heroine in a horror movie, the only one who could see the creeping paralysis infecting everyone about me.

'Babies *are* boring,' my friend Laura told me when I complained to her on one of our phone calls. 'Kids don't get interesting until they can talk.' But when I had the chance to test this theory – after everyone I knew had partnered up – I found toddlers just as tedious as well as quite a bit stickier. As for their effect on anyone around them, it was worse than babies. The sound of the voices of people I knew well modulating instantaneously into sing-song banalities made me cringe.

It seemed that, in the presence of children, most adults' brains flicked into another mode, one I simply didn't have. For a while, it amused my friends that I couldn't talk to children in anything other than my regular voice. 'You sound like you're reading them the *Financial Times*,'

Ben once told me. But I couldn't help it, and I saw no reason to mask my disappointment if my skirt was grabbed at with chocolatey hands, or my conversation interrupted for the 15th time. I felt no compulsion to engage with, or entertain, the small figures who had appeared in my social circle without invitation.

Tom and Laura were accepting of the fact that I didn't fall in love with their respective children and understood that when I visited, I wanted to reconnect with them, not spend time in a painful three-way conversation about which superpowers the Mighty Pups have. Others, however, rolled their eyes and told me my standoffishness was a pose. One person got angry. 'Deciding that an entire subsection of humanity isn't worth your time doesn't make you cleverer than everyone else,' she said. 'It makes you a bigot.'

I was a bit shaken by this criticism and worried she might have a point. After that I stayed quiet about how I really felt and I got better at faking. I wouldn't say I went into my encounters with children any more open-minded, and I still avoided mass gatherings of them, including any birthday parties that celebrated a single-digit number. But I learned to stifle my weary sigh at the sound of their piercing screams and to appear more interested in 30-piece jigsaws.

Was I less womanly than other people of my sex?

I didn't linger on the idea but I couldn't avoid it entirely – especially as time passed and the broodiness I'd expected to settle on me one day, like a religious vocation or nuclear fallout, never arrived. If cultural markers were to be believed, then by my late twenties I should have been unable to behold a baby without a secret swell of maternal longing and by my mid-thirties I should have been walking around to a background hum of unfulfilled fertility. Was my biological clock broken? Or had someone just forgot to set the alarm?

Either way, I suspected that it had made my singleness a lot simpler – possibly even less frightening. While I was perfectly capable of envying many of the things that couples had – 24-piece dinner services, expensive vacuum cleaners, houses with their own front door – I didn't suffer the gratuitous added pain of childlessness. My desire for a husband, however deep, wasn't amplified by the belief that I would make a great mum. Nor was it attached to a terrifyingly arbitrary time limit.

Kate had always known she wanted children – two, ideally – and yet I'd never stopped to picture it because I'd always thought of our lives running in perfect parallel. (I was the only girl I knew who had ever fantasized about being a bride in a double wedding, like the one at the end of the BBC's *Pride and Prejudice*. I was gutted when this was finally off the table.)

Now, the weak light of the bulb in our parents' bedroom reflected two smudgy outlines in the mirror that hung over our mother's dressing table. People could usually tell we were sisters from a single look – our eyes, our colouring, our mannerisms all gave us away. We were alike in far more ways than we were different. On the phone, even our dad couldn't tell our voices apart.

Our passions and personalities coincided too. Sure, Kate was a little more cautious, and I was wound a bit tighter. But we were equally talkative and excitable; we both enjoyed an audience. Our shared love of theatre and movies and American sitcoms was channelled into a similarly obsessive method of critique that ruined them for anyone else. Our sense of humour was so perfectly in tune that my sister's were the only Netflix recommendations I ever needed.

So it was strange to think there could be anything we didn't share. As we stood suspended in her secret, the big news we would swallow down the moment we left the room, I had a moment of vertigo. My sister had already overtaken me on the prescribed route to adulthood – and now she was disappearing into the distance, down a path I wasn't going to follow.

When my mother learned that she would finally be realizing her dream of becoming a grandmother, her

reaction was not unpredictable. A strategist to her core, she turned her laser focus and supertanker momentum towards every aspect of her grandfoetus's future. Within a couple of days she knew the opening hours and Ofsted reports of all the nearest preschools; by the 20-week scan, she was arguing with her son-in-law about universities. It seemed likely this baby would have a pension portfolio before I did. On the plus side, the candle burns were already yesterday's news.

Sunday lunch at my parents' place was a family tradition; our mum's roast dinners were an indulgence it was hard to turn down. We now discovered that there was no dinner topic that couldn't, and wouldn't, be redirected to the imminent arrival.

'I can't believe Brexit is happening,' I might say. 'I've started having actual nightmares about it.'

'Actually, Kate, I've been thinking you should buy some swaddles, it's the best way to get them to sleep through the night.'

Or: 'I'm thinking of quitting my job and going to live in America permanently.'

'That reminds me – Justin, you need to look into how soon you can get the baby a passport . . .'

Over the course of the pregnancy, our get-togethers became full-scale planning meetings, conducted in an impenetrable jargon. Feeding pillows, toilet locks,

vibrating bassinets, burp cloths, amniotic fluid – alien words and concepts dominated the conversation. It was as if I had suddenly discovered that everyone in our family was bilingual, except me.

The language was a symbol, an outward indication of an inward truth: our family was reorienting itself around the newcomer. Invisible and unknowable, the creature in Kate's belly was now pulling our strings like a puppeteer-savant. And if its influence was this strong before it achieved full corporeal embodiment, I could only imagine what power it was going to wield when it finally broke out.

The coming of the baby wasn't just going to change what we talked about but what we did, how we operated, even who we were. Priorities were shifting, doors closing. A few months earlier, Justin and Kate and I had gone to Madrid for a long weekend of strong drink (Justin claimed it was research for his bar). We had stayed out every night sampling giant gin and tonics, mitigating our morning hangovers with custard tarts. It had felt like a blueprint for future holidays together; now I knew it was the Musketeers' last hurrah.

So much of my adult life had been spent celebrating other people's milestones – their engagements and weddings and mother- and fatherhoods – that I'd taken my own state to be one of limbo, in which nothing would really change until I found a mate. Now I discovered

I was wrong. Something was coming that wasn't just going to make new demands of me but bestow on me a new identity. It was an identity I hadn't asked for but, short of renouncing my family ties and moving to another country, it was one I couldn't avoid. I was about to become – and there really was no pleasant way to say it – a maiden aunt.

The phrase had first dropped into my mind a day or two after Kate shared her news. It landed gracelessly, with a judder of self-pity. Even unspoken, it had a sharpness that made the insides of my mouth water. I tried to laugh it away – how Victorian, how absurd! – but it didn't respond to humour. It just sat there, making its sorrowful presence felt.

Spinsterdom had felt, until now, entirely theoretical. I was single but not hopelessly so, and in this light my continuing independence seemed spunky and intrepid, quite possibly the only cool thing about me. Kate's baby-to-be pricked my complacency. The little world in which I moved was rearranging itself without my input or my consent. It tilted its face towards the next generation like a sunflower chasing the sun. Or, perhaps, a dilated cervix. I'd never paid attention in biology class and wasn't completely sure of the process.

Either way, I was feeling more than a little spare. My dad accidentally added to the effect one night at my parents' cottage, when Kate, Justin and I were all staying over. It was a chilly evening and, as we finished our game

of Trivial Pursuit, I grumbled about how cold our rooms were likely to be. 'Yes,' teased Dad, 'and at least the rest of us have someone else to warm us up.'

It was strange that an addition to our family unit should make me feel more solitary. But being an aunt didn't sound like a position of intimacy or something that would bind me closer to anyone. If anything, my new title seemed to push me out of the frame with its knight's move – one up, two across. It relegated me to the sidelines and aged me in the process. It also came with a trio of instantly depressing modifiers: ancient, distant and, of course, spinster.

'You'll be Auntie Em, like in *The Wizard of Oz*!' my mum declared gleefully. I felt my hair greying at the prospect.

Back in London, my familiar routine and surroundings warped into something less desirable, less optimistic. I had always taken pride in my last-minute life. Dressing each day for the possibility I might not be home for dinner. Owning a fridge that was usually empty of everything except lemons, limes and an emergency bottle of champagne. Now my rituals began to ring a little false.

One evening on my way home, I stopped in at Sainsbury's for my regulation what-the-hell-am-I-going-to-eat-tonight shop. It was a big store and always quiet after seven, so I took my basket to one of the empty conveyor belts. As I watched the contents scroll past the

matronly cashier, I saw what she saw. A packet of cashew nuts, a single tomato, an individual sachet of hoisin sauce and a nub of ginger so small it was probably wastage. My eyes misted. If my literature degree had taught me anything, it was how to recognize pathos.

I packed my sad little items into my bike pannier and cycled them home. I carried them up my four flights of stairs to the kitchen. I cooked an under-seasoned stir-fry and ate it in front of a gruesome crime drama. I realized that I couldn't remember how it felt to be kissed. I went to bed alone.

And there I lay, staring at the sloping eaves and the whitewashed woodchip wallpaper that I had slept under for over a decade. The bedroom décor had never been given the same attention as the rest of the flat. The walls were pink. Most of the furniture in it was random second-hand junk I'd picked up on Freecycle in my youth – mismatching pieces hidden under equally mismatching tablecloths, at least one of which had been borrowed from my parents and never returned. I had never bothered to replace any of these things because who else had to look at them anyway?

The bed hadn't had a secondary occupant since Matt. And yet I habitually restricted myself to a sliver of mattress on the left-hand side. The rest of the bed – it was a king-size, for Christ's sake – lay barren. I looked on this pillowy

wasteland and tried to picture the guy who might one day inhabit it.

He would be divorced, almost certainly, or at least have a long-term relationship under his belt. Someone whose past would be a little intimidating, either way – I knew I was unlikely to find anyone else with as little relationship history as me at this stage in the game. He might even have children. I wouldn't want to hang out with them, of course, so he'd have to be the kind of dad who wasn't involved in his kids' lives. I instantly judged him for his callousness and irresponsibility.

OK, he definitely didn't have kids. He couldn't *want* them either, because there was no way I was going to find the love of my life and instantly subject myself to a passion-killing pregnancy. I was damned if I was going to miss out on my lost years of romance for an irreversible parental commitment. Nor was I prepared to postpone the baby-making and become a first-time mum in my mid-forties.

No chance he'd be rich, of course – I had never fancied a successful, wealthy man without immediately being introduced to his spouse. So, then: I was looking at a struggling divorcé with as few nurturing qualities as myself. My enthusiasm for the project was already waning.

I couldn't even come up with a fantasy guy I wanted to be with. And an idea I had been successfully ignoring for years finally penetrated the barrier of my conscious mind.

Maybe my singleness wasn't a temporary arrangement. Maybe I wasn't 'pre-married' at all.

This sharp stab of a thought punctured my defences; hope drained out of me. It was a possibility that changed everything. No longer was I living in a starter home, something I would trade up when the right guy came along. My little flat wasn't an exploratory vessel, charting a course through a sea of opportunity. It was the stationary long-term container of a 38-year-old woman who hadn't had a boyfriend in years. And somewhere she would likely be trapped until the end of her life.

I usually refused to worry for the single women I knew. Much of this was based on personal comparison: I could always identify ways in which they were more physically attractive than me, or had a more winning personality, or knew how to navigate their preferred gender better. I was always sure they were going to score an amazing partner and they usually proved me right.

But there were exceptions. There always seemed to be one, in any social group, who was doomed to struggle, and though her friends told her they could never understand why, they had their private thoughts on the matter.

I wondered if I was that woman.

It dawned on me that even my mother had stopped asking me about guys. One happy byproduct of the babymania was that she had never demonstrated less

interest in my private life. She hadn't even noticed that the internet dating subscription she had bought me for my last birthday had lapsed (I was grateful that I no longer had to make up grey-sounding guys with major personality flaws). There was every chance my mum had moved on and was now mentally organizing her grandchild's future wedding.

The pain I felt at this realization was perverse. I had been angry and sore at the pressure on me to find a boyfriend. Now the thought that people might have given up all together hurt just as much.

Perhaps this was the true reason that the phrase maiden aunt had haunted me. It wasn't the outdated blast of Victoriana that bothered me, the image of a busybody with a sharp nose and a bonnet that had seen better days. It was the implication of finality. It was the fear of being consigned to the box of hopeless causes.

The day after my grim epiphany, I stayed on the sofa, surfing Freeview for feelgood sitcoms. One of the channels was showing repeats of the American version of *The Office*, which I usually found the perfect pick-me-up. Halfway through one of the episodes, however, two of the show's terminal failures admitted to each other they suspected they had missed their chance at love.

I picked up my phone and texted my sister: *I'm watching* The Office *and Michael and Andy are talking about how they*

want to get married and don't think they ever will and now I feel like them except more loser-y because I'm a real person and they're not.

Three blinking dots appeared immediately, as if I'd sent up a telepathic bat signal.

Michael is definitely older than you. And he ended up with lovely Holly.

More dots, then: *Also, you're not actually a loser.*

This was nice. Kate usually *loved* calling me a loser. More dots.

We don't have any control over when we meet the perfect person, just like we don't have any control over tornados or the lottery. I'm sorry it's sucky for you to have to wait though, I wish I could speed it up.

She really was the best.

And even if you never found the guy of your dreams, you'd still have an amazing life because you're an amazing human being.

What

the

actual

fuck.

My sister was prepared to admit, even in the future conditional tense, that it might never happen?

I threw my phone across the room.

CHAPTER 8

Marisa and I had a lot of fun in our thirties. We adventured through the outh of France in a roofless MG, sporting Thelma and Louise headscarves. We hired staging and put on a six-hour music festival in my back garden, and my neighbours thanked us rather than calling the police. We discovered that an older gentleman living on my street was a dealer in antique spirits and shamelessly befriended him so that we could drink 100-year-old negronis in his company.

My Kiwi pal consistently made me feel like one of life's big winners. Then she fell hard for a guy who worked in a bike repair shop. Things got semi-serious and they decided to try living in New Zealand for six months and see where it led. They split up before they even found a house but Marisa stayed on, moving back with her folks, reconnecting with friends and places she'd been separated from for over a decade.

It wasn't easy to maintain a long-distance friendship with someone in a country so close to the international date line. I would wake in the morning to a message telling me she was a bit down and by the time I reached her, she was out, being cheered up by someone I'd never heard of before. Her departure to the other side of the world had the jagged

edge of a break up. And even though I was now accustomed to the pre-ordained migratory pattern of people my age upping and leaving me, I couldn't help but feel that the universe just didn't intend me to have anyone special.

There was no suicidal leap into self-pity, however; no deep dive into despond. I had plenty of people to call on, I just didn't know which of them would be available at any given time. When I felt lonely, I scrolled through my phone, leaving a scattering of messages and waiting to see who responded. This friend lottery had the superficial attraction of being a game I couldn't lose, since I liked all these people in the first place.

Come the winter I joined a scratch choir, formed to sing some carols at a Christmas service. Among the altos were a pair of friends called Heather and Katie who I found indistinguishable. They were equally petite, with black shoulder-length hair and big eyes; they both wore slightly standoffish expressions that reminded me of Enid in *Ghost World*. For a good while I confused each of them with the other, asking about recent holidays they'd not been on or carrying on long conversations about a job they didn't have. Neither of them ever called me out on it but by the time I finally learned their names, I had good reason to feel a little nervous around them.

They were younger than me, as were many of the people I was getting to know these days. My peers no

longer stayed out for post-work drinks – they had people to feed, bathe or read stories to. At the church I attended, the thirty-somethings tended to be heavily involved in the Sunday school, a plague pit of slime-covered plastic that I was careful to avoid. I found myself gravitating instead towards the single folk with the most intriguing-sounding backgrounds. Bledi, an Albanian optometrist. Nicola, who gave up a dream job in publishing to train as a management accountant.

Heather had worked as a policy advisor at City Hall and was now a civil servant in the Department for the Environment, Farming and Rural Affairs. She had grown up in Birmingham and Milton Keynes and, as far as I knew, her closest tie to the land was the Barbour jacket she bought when she got the job. She was, however, bright as a spark and sharp as a needle, and her sense of humour was correspondingly electric and stinging.

Once the choir had fulfilled its remit, belting the descant to 'Once in Royal David's City' and finger-clicking its way through 'Santa Baby', Heather and I had fallen into a couple more musical endeavours. It turned out that, like me, Heather played the violin and she had suggested we take a bash at some duets. We blu-tacked the sheet music to my living room wall and sight-read through some Bach together. Convinced we were nailing it, we recorded ourselves on her iPhone, only to listen

back to a chaotic cliff-tumble of notes that suggested our classical days were behind us.

After that, Heather became a frequent visitor and her social calls left me with the same kind of glow you might get from a bracing walk in the wind. She was fearless in her opinions and untroubled by their effect on anyone else. Her feminism was far less apologetic than mine – perhaps the nine years between us had an effect on the way we approached the world. When I began my career in sportswriting, my mother advised me to mask my grit under outward displays of grace and gratitude, and to allow my inevitably male bosses to believe that any idea I came up with was originally theirs.

These precepts came directly from her own experience of navigating a legal profession at a time when men were dismissive, resentful and suspicious of female lawyers. It was an atmosphere not dissimilar from the press boxes I encountered when I started out. Heather had no time for pandering, however. She was fed up with the lie that women in the developed world now had all the equality they needed and she was not prepared to hide her frustration to make the people around her more comfortable.

She particularly riled our friend Neil, which was impressive as he was one of the most empathic and even-tempered people I'd ever met. Once, when Heather was on a big kick about Taylor Swift's treatment in the press,

Neil mildly observed that she would probably weather the storm and that there might be better things to get angry about than the injustices facing a mega-rich superstar – a reasonable enough comment since his own job was helping women escape forced marriage.

'That's because the continued vilification of women in the public sphere doesn't affect *you*,' said Heather, tartly. 'You live in a world where man is the default, so of *course* it doesn't seem so important. Even the *pronouns* society uses make us invisible . . .'

I didn't like to go up against her myself; I adopted a more cowardly technique, framing my counterviews as questions and retreating when she knocked them down. But I got a vicarious thrill from watching her in battle and I could imagine, in the corridors of government, plenty of middle-aged men underestimating her elfin look and finding themselves on the wrong end of a forensic takedown. Her boldness also gave me licence to feel some of the grievances I'd kept pent up, fearing that they were nothing to complain about in the grand scheme of things. Maybe it wasn't OK that I hadn't had a pay rise in five years? Perhaps I *should* be pissed off when guys told me I was 'getting a bit high-pitched'?

Neil thought that when we were together, we had a tendency to fixate on the negative, rather than remembering that humans are, on the whole, a decent

bunch just trying to do their best. But the times that Heather felt as if the world was conspiring against her were the times I found myself rooting for her the most. 'She's just frustrated,' I told Neil, 'and I know exactly how she feels.' It was how I had felt in my own twenties, the crushing dread that my potential wasn't being fulfilled and my limited youth would be gone before it was.

Heather worked long hours, took no time in lieu, deferred her holidays for the ease of her managers – all the things I had done at her age. I knew how easy it was, as a single woman, to make work the place you earned your validation. You may have decided, in your post-feminist way, that needing the love of a man or a woman to feel complete was socially conditioned behaviour born of outdated gender stereotyping. But finding self-worth in your job – rising through the ranks, impressing others in your industry – was completely acceptable. After all, you couldn't control whether someone you had a crush on liked you back but you could make yourself indispensable and unrejectable at work.

My very first job in London was working on a website that had been conceived in a hurry during the dotcom bubble. It was an entry-level role as an editorial assistant who was expected to make teas and type up other people's interviews. Within a few weeks of my arrival, the website had run out of investment money and its owner had

made everyone redundant with the exception of Judith, the editor-in-chief, and me, the editorial assistant on a negligible salary that could, presumably, be written off against tax.

Suddenly I was Judith's only employee, her only resource and the only person she could offload to about the fiends who were running the company into the ground. We sat in a large, empty office, surrounded by the detritus of hastily emptied desks, the phones still blinking with unanswered calls, a foosball table mocking us from the break room. Desperately out of my depth, I drifted through these crumbling remains trying to reconstruct what it was that had once been done here.

My task, as I saw it, was to keep the sole remaining survivor of this former civilization alive and well. I focused all my energy on reading Judith's needs. Even if I didn't have the skills to accomplish what she asked of me, I could at least show that I had anticipated it. This lightning apprenticeship in keeping the boss happy shaped the career that followed.

A few years later, working on a print magazine, I found myself elevated to the position of deputy editor. The extra responsibility did make me a little nervous but I discovered that the role fitted me easily. I liked my editor a lot but, even more than that, I liked being someone's right hand. Whatever they needed, I wanted to make it happen.

There was, too, something addictive about the process of creating a magazine. Every month, your designer handed you a flat-plan, its 60 or more empty rectangles representing the blank pages you had to fill from scratch. This took more words, pictures and effort than an outsider could ever believe. It also happened in its own impossibly impractical rhythm. On a monthly publication, you took it far too easy the first week, felt a mounting sense of unease in the second and spent the third furious with yourself that you weren't further along the process. The fourth passed in a blur of activity and exhaustion, ending with a huge hit of adrenalin and a promise that you would never subject yourself to such a last-minute push again.

The cycle was inescapable and compelling: for all its labour pains, I always looked forward to the week we went to press. These were the buzziest hours, the ones that made me feel important, the ones when my boss leaned on me most and I knew that I was the only person who could take the load.

I ended up working for five different editors on three different magazines over a little more than a decade. One of my bosses was such a perfectionist, and deferrer of decisions, that we regularly missed our 6pm print deadline and often worked on till the early hours of the morning. As long as we had the proofs ready and signed off by the time the courier arrived for them first thing we

were safe, but the office containing the proofing printers was behind a courtyard that was locked at midnight. Our Hamburgler efforts to mount the gate and sneak into the building brought me immense joy and the fact that I was literally going over the top for my commanding officer only increased my sense of loyalty.

My hunger for approval was nothing new; it had been there since childhood, informing the way I behaved with my parents, my teachers and anyone in a position of authority. Working for an audience of one definitely exacerbated it, however. The two bosses I admired most were the ones who set themselves the highest standards and were thus the hardest to impress. They were both relatively quiet and contained, and a word of praise from them was a precious jewel. Whenever I received one, I mentally hoarded it, repeating it to myself in the moments before I fell asleep that evening to make sure I captured the exact wording and didn't let it slip from my memory.

But the longer I was a deputy, the less satisfying it became. Part of it, I knew, was personal. No matter how good the office chemistry, there was inevitable heartbreak when you invested so heavily in a work relationship, especially one so one-sided. It hurt that I ceased to be relevant the moment my boss left work for the day, especially as I basked in our joint achievements the way other people celebrate their kids' progress at school.

There was another hard lesson, too. My naïve enthusiasm bore me along for a good while until I learned that I couldn't expect an organization, however well-meaning, to have my individual interests at heart. My diligence was my value – I was a steady hand, a reliable worker, someone who made sure that things got done. But all my attempts to prove myself capable of more – taking the company's management courses, developing new skills – went unrecognized. If anything, making myself more useful only entrenched me further. My workplace owed me nothing more reciprocal than my pay cheque; it was never going to love me back the way I needed it to.

I shared some snippets from my experience with Heather as a kind of warning from her future – at least, that's what I told myself I was doing. Heather didn't actually seem the sort of person who particularly welcomed external advice or invited intimacy. When people were saying goodbyes she stood back a little and stiffened her arms in a gesture that suggested a hug was unlikely. In social settings she was the first to have her phone in her hand and would, if a conversation was boring her, retreat into it altogether.

Left alone, just the two of us, we embraced a comically exaggerated world-weariness and entertained ourselves by listing all the things that pissed us off: people who drove too close to cyclists, the fact that off-licences didn't

do home delivery, the way that mooncups left a trail of absolute destruction in your bathroom.

'Mooncups can fuck right off.'

'And lip gloss.'

'And Gwyneth fucking Paltrow.'

'And Kanye bastard West.'

'And Donald arsing Trump.'

We purged ourselves with expletives. 'What is wrooooong with these people?' Heather would drawl, and I would see her expression of deadpan disgust and burst into laughter.

As the months went on, our lists grew longer and more darkly honest. Managers who took credit for your work. Managers who made a big point of giving you credit for your work but refused to back you up when you asked for a pay rise. Guys who acted like they were fascinated by you at a party and then, after you'd got excited and arranged to meet up for a coffee, gushed about their wife and twins. Guys who were single, took you for multiple coffees, flirted with you on WhatsApp, then told you they were thinking of changing career and asked for an introduction to your boss. Going away with a group and having to share a twin room with someone you didn't know because the couples had all the doubles with ensuites. Being told you couldn't say you were tired because you didn't have kids and you didn't know what tired was. Pitching in for engagement/

hen-do/wedding/baby gifts when the people you bought them for didn't even send a text on your birthday.

I loved our purging sessions. It was a relief to say out loud that there were things I hated, things I envied, things I wanted, things that truly sucked. I had been raised to look on the bright side, to get my head down and try harder when things didn't work out. Count your blessings. Contentment in all things. Now I had found someone with whom I was unafraid to admit to an emotion I'd kept hidden from others – and myself – for a *fuck*ing long time. Which was a potent and not entirely irrational anger at many of the things I could not control and much of the way the world worked.

No one had told me that anger was unproductive or unattractive (or unfeminine) but somehow I had come to believe it anyway. The parts of myself that found life unfair had simmered silently or raged in voices only I could hear. Occasionally they coagulated into a bout of anxiety; sometimes they forced themselves out in tears I didn't understand and quickly put down to hormones.

Mostly they just lurked, ignored, the jangling limbs of a basement horror that wanted more than anything to stamp and scream about minor irritations and personal slights and the utter fucking injustice of the world. I squashed these thoughts as best as I could under a punishing regimen of outward gratitude. What survived of them was

compacted down into bitterness and envy, and harboured as my shameful secret.

Now, with Heather, I had a release. She was a safe conductor of unworthy thoughts and feelings, earthing them through the sofa that formed an L-shaped angle to the telly. I lay on the other sofa, staring up at the chandelier-style light fitting I'd bought when I moved in. It had its own place on my list. Ever since I'd installed a dimmer switch, the bulbs had blown repeatedly and now only two of the seven still worked. I had lived with the inadequate illumination and creepy one-sided shadows for ten years.

'Sometimes I think I don't care as much about other people as normal people do,' I told her. 'Look at Marisa. She's on the other side of the world, I should miss her. But most of the time I've forgotten she even exists.'

'Idiot, you're just getting on with your life. That's what everyone does.'

'Yeah, but my life doesn't require me to make any kind of compromise or sacrifice. I literally don't have to think about anyone except myself. Doesn't that make me selfish?'

'Of course not! You're nice to people. And think about it from the other direction – you don't have anyone helping you out. If you don't worry about what you're going to eat and where you've got to go and how you're going to pay for it all, who is?'

'Yeah.' I wanted to believe her but it felt like an excuse. 'I guess I just think . . . other people seem to be motivated by each other. Like, they do the things they do because they care about someone else. I just do things to please me. I mean, I say I love my friends but I don't actually do anything for them because they don't require me to. So maybe I don't love them, not properly. Maybe because I'm single I haven't developed that side of me.'

'Are you saying you're not capable of loving people?'

'Maybe. Maybe that's *why* I'm still single.'

'Right. Shut up.'

One late-summer day, Heather texted and asked if she could come and stay with me for the weekend. She'd been off work since Monday with a stomach bug and she was fed up with the sight of her own bedroom. Her housemates were away too, so there was no one around to cheer her up or offer sympathy. I told her to come straight over and we could comfort-watch episodes of *Gilmore Girls*. She spent long stretches asleep in the spare room – the next weekend, too. The GP had said she might have IBS and should try a gluten-free diet. I warmed up some chicken soup and she left most of it in the bowl.

After struggling through the next week, she said she'd see the doctor again if she didn't feel better by Monday. Normally, she would have been her own best advocate but

she was so unlike herself that I offered to join her and make sure they were taking her symptoms seriously. It's what my mother would have done – ask questions, take notes, sprinkle the conversation with the words 'second opinion' and 'legal career'. Heather said she'd rather go alone.

When she called at 8.30 on Monday morning, I assumed she had changed her mind but her voice was wobbly and she said she'd been to the doctor already. 'She's sent me to hospital for some tests,' she said. 'I'm in a taxi heading there now. Can you come with me? And maybe bring me some pyjamas?'

I ran around my flat stashing pants (two pairs? one? I went with two), a spare toothbrush and some miniature bottles of fancy shampoo from the back of my bathroom cabinet in a bag. When I arrived at the hospital, a 20-minute cycle ride later, Heather had been taken through to a cubicle in A&E. A nurse pulled back a curtain to reveal her perched on a trolley in a hospital gown and knickers, legs dangling a good distance from the floor. I put an arm round her and asked what was happening. Her eyes were red but she clenched her jaw bravely. 'I don't know but it can't be good, can it?'

We sat and waited as a noisy floor polisher came and went. 'Peaceful,' I said. She rolled her eyes.

Then an upbeat nurse called Dan saw us through to a separate room and said encouraging things about a doctor

coming soon. He took lots of blood, decanting it into various tubes and bottles shaped like whisky miniatures. It was hard for him to find a way into Heather's tiny veins and she squeezed my hand as the needle worked its way into the crook of her elbow. Dan apologized and offered to let her punch him on his way out. 'Do you have a long line of people waiting to do that?' she asked. 'No,' he replied, 'but it's only my second day.'

There was an ECG and a CT scan, and I had to wait outside in the corridor where a poster announced 'Someone gets infected every two minutes', which seemed a really bad advert for the hospital. Then somehow it was lunchtime already and we shared some of a sandwich I'd brought, until a doctor came in – a brusque woman with a European accent who examined Heather and asked questions in an accusatory tone: what did you have for breakfast this morning? Why are you here?

She spoke solely in medical terms and asked Heather if she'd noticed any lymphadenopathy, to which the only possible answer was 'How would I know?' In the middle of a stream of indecipherable sentences, and hardly audible amid the rest of the junk, I heard her drop in the word 'lymphoma', like a piece of litter. I didn't look at Heather. I just stared at this woman, hating her and wanting her to leave.

When she did, a nurse started talking about the

practicalities of getting Heather admitted, 'If it's as serious as we think it is.' I looked at my friend and saw that she was as confused as me. 'I'm sorry,' I said, 'what *do* you think it is?' And she said, yes, sorry, yes, but they suspected cancer, and sorry, yes, it must be a shock. And then she left and I sat on the bed next to Heather, put my arm round the back of her neck and she folded her head into my shoulder and cried. We stayed that way for a long while. 'For fuck's sake,' she said, eventually. 'I don't want to die.'

Her parents were soon on their way back from their holiday in the Lake District, her brother from his job in the City. The interim was a curiously hilarious one – I don't know how we found so much to laugh at. Giggles as we talked about using the diagnosis to get out of stuff: 'So sorry I can't come to your baby shower, I've got cancer.' Proper belly laughs as she was whisked upstairs, backwards, to an ultrasound, the breeze lifting through her robe. Heather had never been a change-in-front-of-others kind of girl, but she embraced a cheerful nudity that day.

I wasn't sure when I'd felt closer to anyone than those strange hours of shared, shocked contemplation. As she was wheeled down corridors in her bed I walked alongside, ready to catch her hand. When we were left alone I stroked her forearm, or drew little circles on her palm, or – when the nurses moved me to the foot of her bed so they could fiddle with IVs – gently pinched her toes.

Only once did my clumsiness nearly disgrace me – I caught myself just before I accidentally sat on her drain bag. Even the drain, the most intrusive thing that happened that day, elicited a surreal pride in her toughness, when the needle going into her side resounded like a staple gun. We watched Calippo-coloured liquid coming out of her stomach and filling the bag at her side, and it was weird and gross and it was funny too.

The consultant – a man with an air of compassionate authority and a very handsome set of features, who Heather and I quickly decided was our favourite – warned us that day of what was to come. A lot of tests, a lot of waiting for results, a week or so that would feel like it went on forever until they could confirm a diagnosis. And he said that because she was young, they would be fighting hard for her; he used phrases like 'new treatments' and 'clinical trials' that made me secretly worry because this didn't seem like we've-caught-it-early kind of talk.

Heather's first couple of months in hospital were physically traumatic. Vital procedures did not go smoothly; she was often too sick for visitors. The few times I did see her, her fragile frame was hollowed out and her fighting spirit was extinguished. The only useful thing I could do for her was act as an official news channel, disseminating updates to friends, colleagues and insurance companies

while she and her parents focused on her health.

This seemed like a task well suited to my abilities and optimistic demeanour, so it was a surprise to find it as painful as I did. The thought of my fragile friend suffering alone was something I found unbearable. Telling her flatmates about the diagnosis, I lost control of my facial muscles and found myself fighting down a hideous grin; I had to fake a bathroom emergency and leave the room. Other times, I felt defensive at the most well-meaning questions, afraid that talking about the situation somehow diminished her and superstitious of expressing any hope.

Once Heather was stable enough to leave hospital between treatments, I had a role which I enjoyed far more. Her condition still needed constant supervision, so her parents took her home to Milton Keynes and my job became Chief Distractor, a sort of muted court jester who showed up with DVDs, board games and an imperviously upbeat attitude. We sat at the kitchen table doing jigsaws or in the living room under blankets watching *Friends*. We made beef bourguignon and lasagne and ate ice cream and celebrated the fact that she was officially authorized to get as fat as she could.

Her parents had put their lives on hold while they cared for her. Heather persuaded them to take a break and visit some family for the weekend if I was there to – her word – 'babysit'. I was to take her temperature twice a day and

drive us straight to the hospital if there was anything that might indicate infection. One Friday evening, we half-watched a movie until she said she was tired and went to bed. On Saturday morning, I padded around the kitchen quietly, waiting for her to come down for some breakfast.

I reminded myself that she needed lots of rest but by mid-morning I was quietly panicking that I hadn't seen or heard from her so I took a cup of coffee up to her room. She was awake, curled like a kitten in the middle of the double bed, surrounded by a cloud of duvet and pillows. I remembered the first couple of weeks of her illness and how she had complained about my mattress. The thinner she'd got, the more cushioning she needed.

'You look like the Princess and the Pea,' I joked.

She took the coffee without speaking. I swung myself onto the bed next to her.

'Did you sleep OK?'

'No.'

A cold fist clutched at my stomach. 'Shall I get the thermometer?' My hand instinctively reached for her forehead. She knocked it away.

'I don't feel ill,' she said, moodily. 'I just feel like someone's who got cancer.'

'I'm sorry,' I said.

'Yeah, well. We're all sorry.'

'I wish I could take it away.'

'Everyone says that. But they can't. This is happening to *me*.'

'Do you want a hug?'

'No.'

We sat in silence. I battled the urge to say something positive, knowing it would just piss her off more. I couldn't help myself.

'Your mum said the last test result was good?'

'It wasn't good, it just wasn't *bad*. They can't tell me whether I'm getting any better. I feel like I'm constantly waiting for the next thing to go wrong.'

'Is there anything we could do right now to take your mind off it?'

'Thanks, but you don't have to manage me.'

Oof. Still, I probably deserved it.

'Shall I go away for a bit?'

To my surprise, she shook her head. I leaned back against the headboard and tried not to glance over. When I did, her jaw was set and she stared ahead fiercely.

'I just lie awake thinking, what if this is it? What if this is all I get?'

I laid a hand on her back.

'It's not fair, you know? It's just not fucking *fair*.' She curled up against my shoulder and I held onto her until she fell asleep. Then I concentrated on wiping the tears from my cheeks before they could reach her.

CHAPTER 9

'Is this your mid-life crisis, then?'

Bledi stood in front of my recent purchase, ruining the moment. He rarely bothered to make a distinction between his private thoughts and his public utterances, and I was used to his bluntness. It only hurt when he was right.

The teal-blue MGB in front of us did not appear to take offence. It crouched passively, its grille and headlamps connecting to form a benign expression that was not quite a smile; the sweep of fins to the backlights added the suggestion of perkiness. To serious car lovers, it was nothing special: a decent example of a mass-produced two-seater, not rare enough to merit notice nor well-preserved enough to be of value. To me, however, it was the embodiment of a long-held promise and a piece of borrowed glamour. It was the first car I had ever owned.

Having spent the entirety of my adulthood in London, always within a short walk of a train or a tube station, driving was a holiday experience for me. In my regular daily life, cars were an irrelevance. I was a confident all-weather cyclist. I even loved the comically slow London buses. A meandering cross-town journey to the West End could inspire genuine bliss if it gave me an hour of hassle-free reading on the top deck.

It wasn't that I didn't like driving. In fact, it was just the opposite. Driving was a pleasure I kept sacred, a whim to be indulged on rare occasions, not to be ruined by rush-hour traffic or attritional parking games at Homebase.

The functionality and convenience of a car never tempted me; I was, however, a sucker for the aesthetic. Since the day I gained my licence as a teenager, I had pictured myself darting around the countryside in a cute little open-top number, a vision I never shook. It represented the person I'd one day like to be: chic and adventurous, free of the mundane concerns of cost or practicality. The day I owned that car would be the one my dreams had all come true.

But now I was nearing 40 and I still wasn't that person. What was I really waiting for? Someone to sit in the passenger seat, maybe, or someone to shoulder the cost with me? It wasn't a huge extravagance, after all. Perhaps I was a little afraid of external judgements – what looked girlishly carefree in a twenty-something might make an older woman seem desperate or deluded. In other words, what Bledi said.

In the end, it wasn't a sense of goals achieved or wishes fulfilled that triggered the purchase but a patch of disappointment. After five years in the same role, I was yearning for something in my life to change – to feel that I was heading somewhere, not just drifting aimlessly.

I ventured to job interviews with high hopes and left feeling small and insignificant. In one particularly humiliating episode, the editor didn't even invite me inside to the company's offices; she just asked her questions in front of the reception desk as bike couriers shuffled past. At my own office, I was the first to volunteer for whatever secondments and side projects came up. Wherever they took me, they always deposited me back in the same place.

So perhaps my Albanian friend had a point – maybe the car *was* a horrible cliché. I couldn't even keep it in London where I lived. The driver's side door didn't lock, and if it had, a joyrider still wouldn't need to take more than a Stanley knife to the folding vinyl roof to let themselves in. Plus, the car was slung so low that every speed bump scraped the exhaust with the sound of an angle grinder.

As a result, few of my friends had actually laid eyes on the MG in the months since I'd bought it. It languished at a stables near to my parents' place where I rented a spot in a barn for a tenner a month. In the first few weeks, I failed to notice the birds' nest in the rafters directly above my parking place and returned to find my pride and joy graffitied with grime, the black canvas of its roof now a Jackson Pollock of pigeon poop. As if in revenge for that humiliation, the car routinely refused to start without at least 20 minutes of coaxing and begging, during which the ignition made strangled noises and the engine threatened

to flood. More than once I planned a weekend of coasting around the countryside but ended up borrowing my mum's Mini while my own car went back to the local mechanic.

And yet, the purchase still brought me a stubborn joy. Not just me, either. Heather soon had a deep affection for the MG because, as she convalesced, we would take it out for little drives and she could enjoy a rush of fresh air when she wasn't feeling strong enough for a walk. Factory fresh in 1972, the car was six years older than me and if we attempted anything more than a firm 65mph the windows began to rattle so violently I worried they might just fall out. I didn't mind driving slower – being so low to the ground made even moderate speeds feel fairly hair-raising.

We christened the car Lady Agatha – Aggie to her friends. Like the redoubtable aunt of Bertie Wooster in P G Wodehouse's novels, she was ageing, demanding and could be perversely disagreeable. Her light-tan seat covers were cracked; the walnut veneer on the dashboard was less than skin deep. There were spots on the chrome and bubbles of rust under the paintwork. The wide wooden steering wheel looked great until you had to use it to turn and found it as unyielding as the lid on a particularly stubborn pickle jar.

Her name also evinced one of my favourite Evelyn Waugh characters – Agatha Runcible, the anarchic Bright

Young Thing of *Vile Bodies,* who gets into a sequence of scrapes before finding herself an accidental competitor in a motor race. It was this Aggie I had thought of as I sat on a steep grass bank next to the A421 between Bedford and Cambridge on a late-autumn day. The 1800 cc engine had let me get halfway through a two-hour journey to Norfolk before deciding, on this fast, downhill stretch of dual carriageway, to conk out entirely and without warning.

One moment I was barrelling along with the roof down and a song in my heart. (The stereo still didn't work – an internal soundtrack was the only musical accompaniment available.) Then suddenly, after the smallest of noises – more of a whimper than a bang – the accelerator stopped working. I stamped on it several times just to check. The car was losing speed fast and the articulated lorry behind me grew terrifyingly large in my rear mirror, playing a dramatic horn crescendo as an overture of doom.

A 1972 MGB does not have hazard lights and even if it did, I wouldn't have had the time or sangfroid to look down at the dashboard and locate them. Instead, I took my arms off the wheel and waved them in an arc above my head, hoping that this might be the universal semaphore signal of distress. I just had time to wonder how high the lorry's axles were above the ground and what it would feel like to be crushed under them before the monster vehicle threw itself into the outside lane and thundered away, horn

still blaring with Wagnerian fury. I pulled over onto the hard shoulder, scrambled out of the car and flung myself onto the bank.

And still, I forgave Agatha for my near-death experience as well as the ensuing hour sat by the roadside with a blanket and thermos, waiting for a tow. I had, I reasoned, expected too much of her. For all her faults, she still made me happier than anything I had owned; no other object had ever had such an instant and outward effect on my mood.

It was, partly, an exhibitionist appeal. With her vintage blue coat and indolent purr, she was a car from a movie, or at least an episode of *Morse*. Her sleek, slim-hipped contours and her pert little trunk attracted stares in a way my own never had. In the rear mirror, I often saw men stopped still on the pavement, following us with their gaze, talking about us in our wake. But even when no one was looking, Aggie made me feel special.

I only had to slide into the driver's seat and let out the clutch to be transported into another world, where the weather was always fine, money was never an object and a valet was waiting to take my bags at the end of the journey. I even dressed more smartly when I went driving; Aggie's own stylishness demanded that I lift my game. Jeans and jacket were replaced with a skirt and overcoat, a scruffy beanie with a leather helmet and gloves.

I didn't need an excuse or a plus-one to drive out in Aggie – she was an adventure and a companion in her own right. That empty passenger seat beside me? That was a statement of glamorous independence and infinite romantic possibility. And I, meanwhile, could be anyone I wanted – not just a 38-year-old singleton with career frustrations and a sense that my life was stalling while everyone else's raced ahead. Cocooned in my capsule, cloaked in a miasma of petrol fumes, I felt like a heroine from a bygone era – Grace Kelly, Amy Johnson or, if I was feeling particularly cartoonish, Penelope Pitstop.

Right now, Aggie was parked in front of a wisteria-covered cottage, the kind that stretches the meaning of the word by having at least half-a-dozen bedrooms and a kitchen with the square-footage of a studio flat. The surroundings suited her: she overlooked a former croquet lawn and an unkempt parterre garden where overgrown lavender wagged violently in the breeze. Scattered around, in lawn chairs and on blankets, were the various single folk who had come here for a relaxing break – some, like Bledi and Neil, who I had known a long while now and others I had barely met before.

Each person had been invited on the basis that someone else in the group thought they were a good egg and as a result we had gelled quickly. Identities were soon established: John, the army doctor, was the fitness freak;

Naomi, the youth worker, was the karaoke queen. Since I had turned up in a classic sports car and was discovered to know the correct ingredients and proportions for making negronis, I was appointed the group lush. It was a role I was more than happy to play, not least because I was given a pass from joining the cooking rota if I took charge of the drinks.

The joke grew as the days went on. While the rest of the band, who were all extremely fitness-conscious, were led in a morning workout by Army John, I wandered down to breakfast in a kimono-style dressing gown carrying the half-empty glass of red wine I'd taken to bed the night before. One day I begged off a hearty hike through the fields to sit in front of the fire reading Virginia Woolf. 'You ought to have a little bell at your side,' said Nicola when she spotted me there. I laughed and told her I'd happily take a sherry. Five minutes later, it had appeared beside me.

This was clearly what people meant by living your best life. I had found the role I was born to play.

I often had fantasies about living in the past. A privileged past, obviously; I wasn't interested in the world my real ancestors inhabited, struggling to keep their dozen children alive in a Welsh mining village or blacking the stoves of an east London slumlord. No, my escapism was born from a heady mix of my two favourite TV shows:

Poirot, starring David Suchet, and *Jeeves and Wooster*, with my comic heroes Fry and Laurie in the eponymous roles.

Both aired on ITV during my highly impressionable teenage years. The lead performances were sufficient to colour me obsessed; the intoxicating production design evoked a universe of its own. I quickly applied myself to the books too, reading and rereading them long after the plots had ceased to hold any surprises. Then came Dorothy L Sayers's Lord Peter Wimsey stories and *Brideshead Revisited* – both the novel and the Anthony Andrews version. From then on, I immersed myself in pretty much anything that involved aristocrats, monocles or spats.

Whenever I was bored of my surroundings – which happened frequently enough – I wished, with a passion that outweighed reason, that I had been born into the pages of these golden-age stories rather than my dull, unglamorous real life. I reimagined myself as one of their characters: a sharp-tongued, shingle-haired socialite with a devil-may-care attitude and a cigarette holder poised seductively between her lips. Her outline was drawn from 1930s detective stories and shaded with the devastating hauteur of a young Katharine Hepburn. She had the wise-cracking wit of Dorothy Parker, the intemperance of Zelda Fitzgerald and the stylistic flair of Elsa Schiaparelli. She was the sum of everything I wished I could be but wasn't.

There was one person who both knew of my secret

self and allowed her one foot in the real world. If anyone understood, enabled and sustained my fantasy life, it was Ben.

It didn't occur to either of us, when we met, that we would one day be as close as we became. The 18-year-old I found myself sitting next to at college events, when places were allocated alphabetically, did not look like someone who wanted to spend time with the preppy product of a private girls' school. He wore a loose-fitting T-shirt with purple-and-white tie-dye spiralling hypnotically to its centre and jeans so shredded they *dared* you to notice them; his hair was scraped back into a ponytail that reached halfway down his back. He read Kahlil Gibran and listened to Led Zeppelin and had spent his sixth-form years playing Dungeons and Dragons with semi-nocturnal friends. He appeared to me to come from another dimension, which was probably the intended effect.

Ben was a fellow English student who was, like me, keen on the theatre. That shouldn't have surprised me as much as it did – he clearly had, after all, both a taste for eye-catching costumes and a punkish disregard for conformity. But it wasn't till I heard him deliver a speech from *Antony and Cleopatra* in class that I realized how deeply he cared about it. He could read Shakespeare better than anyone I had ever met, with an emotion that could punch you in the heart.

The other thing I discovered was that he could make me laugh a lot. I was inclined to be intimidated by the rich public-school kids who ran the college's social affairs and looked down on the rest of us. Ben was intimidated by no one. He was always ready with a single raised eyebrow and the perfect takedown, and by the end of the first year, we were staying up late into the night to write an anonymous gossip column in the college paper.

We got our comeuppance when the overzealous new editor put our names to it and our doors were beaten on by angry young men who'd had their indiscretions publicized. But we weathered the social stigma and took command of the college's drama society, putting on plays together and engineering cast parties whenever I had a new dress I wanted to show off.

Laura and I were living in a flat on the wrong side of college at this time and Ben regularly gave up his own bed and slept on the floor so I didn't have to walk home. I haunted his rooms like a house elf, learning the words to 'Kashmir' and 'Black Dog', campaigning hard for the retirement of a mustard bathrobe whose towelling fabric had worn precariously thin and left risqué holes at crotch level.

The D&D had long disappeared – there was no one else who knew how to play – and the ponytail went next, possibly an admission that it was preventing him getting

the acting roles he wanted, if not the girls. The mustard bathrobe was ceremoniously binned – a few of us wanted to set light to it but were afraid of the noxious fumes it might release – and replaced with a paisley dressing gown that would have pleased Noël Coward.

It suited him. Towards the end of our college days, he started seeing his first boyfriend and quietly came out. I had long since cast us as Noël and Gertie in my mind – or, in our seedier moments, Brian Roberts and Sally Bowles – and that make-believe accompanied us to our first London flat together. It allowed me to envision a squalid little corner of a council block as a den of bohemian sophistication, even when the walls reverberated with someone else's drum 'n' bass and the cooking smells from next door enveloped the living room in a farty cabbage odour.

Ben rarely let the mundane reality of our existence get him down. His moods were more 'artistic' and I secretly enjoyed it when he let his temper loose, thundering his displeasure at an absent acquaintance or picking a fight so he could storm out of the room. He could keep up a sulk for days, then the invisible clouds left without warning and I'd come home to find him cooking us pancakes, jubilantly waving a spatula and wearing nothing but an apron.

We joined an amateur dramatics company on the opposite side of the city and spent considerable amounts

of our time and money travelling there for rehearsals. The rest of it was devoted to seeing shows in the West End and on the South Bank, where we sat in the cheap seats and drank tap water at the interval. In the confines of our home, however, we pretended to a luxury we couldn't afford. This mostly revolved around our drinking habits. Ben had a taste for fine malt whisky and I, having read somewhere that Coco Chanel only drank champagne, decided to embrace the same habit. I managed three weeks before imminent penury forced me to abandon the pose.

We remained committed to these plays of extravagance and threw fancy dress parties even when we couldn't accommodate more than a dozen people at them. Ben had, at some stage, convinced me that a lady never finished her glass of wine – something about it being ill-mannered to look thirsty. From that moment I always left a little well of liquid in the bottom of my glass, a disgracefully wasteful habit, although I did sometimes follow my receptacle to the kitchen and gulp down the dregs when he wasn't looking.

The eternal alliance of the single woman and her gay best friend has proven a hackneyed trope in fiction. It tends to provide the hapless female singleton with a sympathetic ear, an enthusiastic dance partner and a last-minute escort to a black-tie do. God knows, Ben fulfilled all three functions often and willingly. But he was also the person who made me feel that I was whatever I wanted to be.

When he finally left to move in with John, the pair of them were forming their own theatre company. Their basement flat was crowded with props and posters, its shelves lined with books on Shakespeare and set design. I was ready to give up on acting. Ben tried to persuade me to stick at it but I was tired of going straight from work to rehearsals and getting home at 1am. The brief frisson of being someone else on stage no longer made up for it.

But I never lost the thrill of feeling like someone else with Ben. Arriving at their door for a quiet midweek dinner, I'd step inside the door and experience a moment of exquisite pleasure as John took my coat and Ben thrust a perfectly chilled gin and tonic into my hand. And as they did, I felt like the kind of woman I'd always dreamed of being: wanted, loved and fabulous.

At the end of our singles' holiday week, we drove to a nearby stately home. One of the guys, possibly angling for a chance to drive Aggie, suggested that what the infamous lush Emma John really needed was a full-time chauffeur. I said I would be happy to employ him once he had the cap and the uniform; in the meantime, I was going to give Bledi a ride.

For most of the journey, Bledi complained bitterly about the lack of leg room, the non-functioning radio and the fact there was nowhere to charge his phone. But then we

swept through the gates of the manor house and crunched noisily along its gravel drive. Other visitors stood aside as we passed; Aggie was giving the strong impression that we were the owner's personal guests rather than paying customers. 'I can see why you enjoy this,' said Bledi. 'We could pull up in front of the door and no one would stop us!'

The house was grand, the kind that causes an involuntary intake of breath as you step into the entrance hall. A coffered ceiling embossed with the family crest, a marble floor laid out in black-and-white checkerboard, a wooden minstrel gallery with faded gilt edging. We were shuffling demurely through the sequence of rooms, past their series of informational placards, when Naomi, who was some way ahead, called down the corridor to us, 'Come see this! Quick, come look – it's Emma's room!'

A small, panelled library greeted us at the end of the corridor. Its walnut shelves were stuffed with leather bindings; its plaster mouldings decorated with art deco fans. A pair of wingback armchairs were gathered next to an empty grate, within easy reach of a large and well-stocked drinks cabinet. It was just the kind of place for a closed-room murder mystery or a caper with a cow creamer.

We let out a group exhale of appreciation and everyone agreed it was just the place for me. I gazed past a rope cordon to a room I couldn't enter and oak floorboards I would never walk on, breathed in the atmosphere of polished indolence

and dreamed myself among the furniture. There was a postcard of the room in the giftshop; I bought one, not just to remind myself of its elegance but to relive the swell of pride I'd felt as my friends dedicated the place to me.

It had been done with such sincerity and affection; they took vicarious pleasure in my glamorous alter ego, however improbable and ridiculous she was. It was a fiction indulged without irony or malice and I felt grateful, even a little celebrated. I wondered why it meant so much to me to find people who made space for, even encouraged, my silly fantasy.

Perhaps it was because my real-life options felt so narrow. Any hopes for a love life were more distant than they had ever been. They were now so far off, in fact, that even the idea of romance had melted invisibly from my vision. 'Is there anyone interesting?' I'd be asked by someone who hadn't seen me in a while. And I would stare at them blankly, feeling like a person who had just woken up on a lilo and realized they could no longer see the shore.

Sometimes when I found myself moved by the final moments of a romcom – or succumbed to the sexual tension of a passionate soapy drama – the thrill of borrowed electricity would run through me and I'd remember with surprise the lost feelings I was capable of. Sex was not something I gave a lot of thought to. Its absence was a

disappointment, theoretically at least, but most of the time I don't think my body noticed what it was missing.

Maybe my alternate persona, vampy as she was, was a way to feel more of a woman. After all, if I wasn't on my way to being a girlfriend or a wife, where was I heading and who *was* I becoming? I wasn't sure, and it made me feel uneasy and ill-prepared for the future.

There are ways to make singleness a less pitiable state. Be rich, be famous, be intriguing or admirable. Fill your timeline with high achievements or hedonistic pleasures or altruistic works. Prove to yourself and everyone else that your life is a rich and complete one: in other words, that you are better off than the drab marrieds who make up most of the population.

I hadn't the patience to be a saint and I felt too old to party for the sake of it. I wasn't inclined to be a workaholic, either; my career didn't seem destined for any kind of greatness. If there was one thing experience had taught me, it was that I was not the sort of person to whom a setback is a challenge and failure an opportunity. My frustrations at work were leaching my motivation and instead of becoming more determined I was now drifting into the office as late as possible and caring little for the outcome.

So play-acting was, I supposed, a way to escape other people's judgement. If I created a character who dazzled more than I did, I could justify my single existence.

I could borrow the confidence of this spunky sophisticate, someone irrepressibly and unapologetically herself.

It was raining heavily as we left the stately home. Neil and Army John ran back to their cars and returned with umbrellas, and chivalrously walked us to the car park under their shelter. It made me feel like a real lady.

CHAPTER 10

The picture from Justin arrived early on a Thursday morning, on WhatsApp. My sister had always had pale skin but the hospital lighting and the exhaustion combined made her positively ghostly. There was a weary smile on her face and, in the crook of her arm, a wrinkled bundle of blanket, out of which peeked an even more wrinkled face. The accompanying caption announced Isabella Grace and came with a strict injunction not to share the photo on Facebook. (The latter was clearly meant for my mother.)

I hadn't even known my sister was in labour but then, apparently, neither had she. Kate was in the kitchen making spaghetti bolognese when she noticed the twinges. They were so mild she was convinced they were the Braxton Hicks contractions everyone at NCT classes kept talking about and she decided to finish cooking the pasta before she checked. When she finally phoned the hospital, the nurse was relaxed. It didn't sound like the real thing. There was no need to hurry.

So Justin drove Kate over there for a check-up and they waited happily enough at reception until a doctor had become free to take a quick look at her. As soon as she did, she announced that Kate was actually having a baby and rushed her onto the ward. Isabella Grace slid into the

world a very short while after. It was a speedier delivery than we got from the Domino's round the corner.

My parents and I converged on their home that afternoon, so keen to meet the new arrival that we actually beat her to the house. 'Now, just make sure you're *helpful*,' my mother told me, as we waited for their car to pull up. 'They'll all be *very tired*. Make tea *as soon* as anyone asks you. Don't get under their *feet*.'

I bit my tongue.

Kate arrived looking marginally less wan than she had in the photo, carrying the sleeping baby into the house with self-conscious carefulness. I was curious to get a look at this new little creature but another part of me was braced for disappointment. The very few newborn babies I had encountered, in dutiful visits made to friends, had been incalculably ugly and it always seemed that I was the only person who noticed this evident fact. Cooing over the entirely fictitious charms of these grumpy, rumpled fleshballs had required considerable acting skills.

Perhaps that was why I was in no hurry to hold my niece. Instead I obediently headed to the kitchen to put the kettle on and, since my sister had come home ravenously hungry, heated up the bolognese that she hadn't had a chance to eat the first time round. When I returned with the steaming bowl of mince, the atmosphere in the living room was tentative, almost nervous. Something

had shifted, invisibly, in our family dynamic; every one of us was looking to Kate for direction, waiting to take a cue from whatever she needed. Even my mother seemed somewhat subdued.

The woollen cocoon and its pudgy pink contents worked its way round the circle, like pass the parcel, until it landed with me. It was a lot lighter than I expected. The baby's eyes were clamped shut with the passive aggression of a do-not-disturb sign; the twist of her mouth suggested defiance rather than tranquillity. If she was cute, it was only in the way that hairless dogs that look like somebody's granddad were cute. But she was genuinely tiny, a result of being ten days early, and her size moved me. It provoked an indefinable emotion. Not love, particularly. Certainly not broodiness. This was more like a newly awoken determination; I felt curiously fierce and disinclined to hand her back.

My expectations of aunthood were, it is safe to say, minimal. The ecstasies of joy that some of my single friends found in their nephews and nieces had always appeared odd to me, even a bit suspect. Alex, for instance. She was a friend whose experiences and opinions matched mine more closely than anyone else I knew. We had taken the same subjects at college and gone into parallel industries; she had pursued her career with the same wholehearted (possibly misguided) devotion as me.

Alex was the first woman I had met who would passionately advocate that singleness was a nobler and more empowering state than any other, infinitely preferable to settling down with a partner for the sake of it. She was also completely uninterested in having children and, like me, tended to bristle a little in their presence. Together, we would safely and discreetly lament the way we felt forgotten by former friends or ostracized by our family-oriented society. We would also bitch contentedly about the lacklustre parenting skills we witnessed out in the world and the spoilt, ungovernable offspring they produced.

And then her brother had a daughter and Alex became a different person. Not in every aspect – just in regard to the kid. She talked about her as much as if she were her own: her progress, her foibles, the things she said and did, all related with the kind of delirious happiness usually associated with the early stages of romance or hypoxia. I listened to the stories patiently, assuming the novelty of being an aunt would wear off over time. But the older the child got, the keener Alex was to hang out with her.

Perhaps biology's magic wand was more powerful than I gave it credit for. Or maybe I just liked being at the centre of the action. Either way, it was a surprise to me how keen I felt to help out in the weeks after Isabella was born. This instinct was doubly curious since, on the surface, I had no

skills or experience to offer. My mother actually told me to keep away the first time I suggested dropping round for more than a brief visit. 'They'll be trying to establish a pattern of sleeping and feeding,' she said sceptically. 'You'll just add to the chaos.'

But Kate wasn't turning down any offer of assistance, however uninformed or butterfingered it might be. Isabella – Izzy, as she quickly became – was a tortuously slow feeder and would only sleep in someone's arms, which made the nights particularly tough on her mother. My sister now had the haunted, hollow look of an SAS trainee regretting their career choice.

I volunteered to take on some overnight shifts and arrived at the house with nothing more than the two basic tenets of childcare: support the head and don't leave them alone in water. The sex education class at my school had ended abruptly at the crackly VHS showing a harrowing downstairs view of labour and while my stint as a Girl Guide had endowed me with superficial knowledge on a number of practical subjects – navigating by the North Star, building a radio, fashioning a tourniquet from a T-shirt and a splint out of lollipop sticks, etc. – there had been no badge for babycare.

Watching Kate and Justin it became clear that – for all the reading they had done and the Netflix documentaries they'd watched on childhood neurological development –

their childrearing knowledge wasn't much more advanced than mine. On the first afternoon, Kate introduced me to her nappy-change routine and told me not to worry when the baby cried because she would cry whatever I did. That was the extent of my induction.

Apparently, parenting operated on the same educational principle that my medical friends spoke of during their hospital training:

See one,

Do one,

Teach one.

Within a few hours, I had absorbed more information about babies than in my previous 20 years of technical fertility – for instance, that getting a baby out of their onesie was much simpler than wrangling their spongy limbs back into it. Or that you could take longer re-attaching the poppers on a sleepsuit than completing a Rubik's Cube but still end up with one trouser leg flapping half-open.

As for getting the kid to sleep, if there was a trick to it, no one in the house had yet fathomed it. I watched as Kate, then Justin – then Kate again, then Justin a bit more – walked the wailing package round and round the living room, bouncing it up and down in increasingly tired arms. Sometimes the noise emanating from inside settled to a whimper and then – if they were lucky and never

stopped moving – reverted to a pattern of shallow little rasps. Sometimes it didn't and they were still walking an hour later.

Under these circumstances, the mere fact that I had functioning elbows made me a useful addition. Since none of Kate or Justin's baby-soothing techniques was notably more effective than any other, I experimented with my own. My most successful innovation was to take Izzy to the dimly lit hallway and make my way up and down it with a series of lunging, swooping steps that ultimately belonged to the Ministry of Silly Walks. These burned out my thighs after half an hour but sometimes by then they succeeded in lulling her into unconsciousness. Either she liked the exaggerated bobbing motion or her poor little brain was just overwhelmed by the sensation, preferring to shut down the way mine would have done if forced on a bungee jump.

However hard it was getting the baby to sleep, it was still easier than keeping her that way. She had an ability to stage a sudden comeback from oblivion that would have impressed the hardiest horror villain. It didn't matter how serene she looked in your arms – somehow, across the desert miles of dreamland, she could still sense the moment you attempted to manoeuvre your weary muscles onto the sofa or, if you were really that foolish, tried to lay her down in her cot.

There was no more high-stakes moment than the handover. My 4am shifts began with Kate standing over me, hissing my name malevolently and, when that didn't work, shoving me with her foot to wake me up. Justin was usually asleep next door after a long day's work and an arduous baby-quieting turn of his own. Standing in the dark, a bolt of adrenalin coursing through my body, I braced myself with my back leg and held my breath as Kate carefully tipped the baby from her arms into mine. It felt as if we were handling six pounds of Semtex, primed and hard-wired.

From the bedroom, I made the hazardous journey downstairs, softening my knee joints to avoid creaking the floor. The controlled descent onto the sofa was the most dangerous moment of the entire operation, thighs and stomach muscles busting with the unaccustomed effort as they lowered me in a graceless squat. Once down, I knew I was stuck in position until the next feed – that even the slightest shift of my body would spell disaster and ruin everyone's night. I once made the mistake of failing to locate the TV remote before I sat down. Twice I made a bid for it and had to give up when Izzy's eyelids started to flicker. That was a long two hours of contemplating the wall.

And yet, those times trapped on the sofa were some of my favourite. The sensation was intoxicating: Izzy's

soft weight resting on my chest, her puckered little mouth breathing quietly near my face. At such moments, a sense of satisfaction would creep through my bones and although my achievements were undeniably great – behold my ninja stealth! witness my nurturing manner! – this wasn't a feeling born of self-esteem. It was, instead, a strange pride that seemed to attach to Izzy herself – or maybe to come from her, I wasn't sure.

Within a couple of months of Izzy's arrival, however, I departed for another country. Or, to be more accurate, a succession of other countries. I had finally had enough of my office job. The company was offering redundancies; I took one, reasoning that my life was not going to change until I changed it myself. My vague and short-termist plan was to travel, and to write, and to write about travel – at least until I ran out of money, which would probably take a year or so.

In the past, my trip-planning had been less concerned with drawing up a list of dream destinations than finding people to holiday with. There was little point agonizing over which continent to visit or choosing between four-star hotels that looked almost identical from their websites when it might take weeks, if not months, to plot how many of my friends had vacation days left, which of them could afford to go further than Norfolk and who from those was

already secretly committed to a group trip I hadn't been invited on but would very much like to have been.

By the time I was in my mid-thirties, there was barely a friend who I hadn't been on holiday with. Companionship was, to me, the most vital ingredient of travel; the thought of being alone and far from home was a waking nightmare. No one to eat with, explore with, unpack your experiences with at the end of the day – what kind of hell was that and why would anyone choose it?

And then I'd decided to make a journey to North Carolina, a part of the US I had never been to before. It was born of an overwhelming urge to visit the South and to listen to the bluegrass music I'd been discovering in its native setting. None of my usual companions were available to tag along on this private quest – at least, that's what they told me – so the choice was to go alone or not at all. And I really, really wanted to go.

Even after I'd talked myself into the trip, it still seemed tremendously sad and lonely to be in another country without a friend. Whenever I tried to picture it – sitting in a restaurant eating my dinner alone or spending an entire day without talking to anyone – I teared up. Before I left, I triple-checked that my return flight was changeable and promised myself that, at the first hint of melancholy, I would fly home. There was no need to be a hero over the cost of a plane ticket and I wouldn't even book myself a

hotel room for more than the first night. The entire venture was underwritten with the acceptance that I might abort at any moment.

On the flight to Charlotte, an overly friendly passenger in the seat next to me called Diane bludgeoned me into conversation, offered to introduce me to her friends and followed through on that promise the moment we landed. It was my first experience of the irresistible, juggernaut force of Southern hospitality, but nowhere near my last. The first time I ate lunch in a diner, a couple further along the counter invited me to slide down and join them. 'You've come all the way here ... alone?' they asked, and almost immediately followed up with an offer to show me around the town.

Being alone and eager for company, I was quick to accept all similar overtures. Whatever straitjacket of inhibitions I had worn as a Londoner – a tendency to avoid eye contact in public, a bristling irritation when people invaded my 'personal space' – began to loosen. Some of my own, innate qualities enjoyed a new and fruitful bloom. A naïve enthusiasm that had required damping down ever since I reached adulthood – particularly in the urbane, cynical setting of my home city – paid off with instant connections; by the end of the first week, I'd been invited to family meals and days out, even to stay in people's guest rooms.

Apparently I was well-suited to travelling stag in America – an uncloaked eagerness to make friends simply wasn't a source of embarrassment here. When I returned to the UK and told others about my trip – the people I'd stayed with, the miles I'd covered, the random banjo player I'd dated along the way – they were impressed. Laura and Ally told me I was brave but it didn't feel that way; that description somehow missed the point. Bravery implied I had faced down fear or danger and my travels had posed neither. What they *had* done was shown me an environment where something that came very easily to me – talking to strangers – became a previously unrealized superpower.

In the years that followed, testing the theory, I took more trips alone and whenever I did, good things happened. A lasting friendship with a Latvian journalist was formed on a long weekend in Riga; in a tiny Trinidadian village, I was invited for tea by the mother of the West Indies cricket captain. The world seemed to be revealing a different side of itself, one where the unusual and unexpected could, and did, happen.

And so I began to seek out assignments that would take me overseas. Without commitments, or a long-term strategy, it wasn't hard to find piecemeal work that would keep me moving. This new approach to work led to a trip to Asia to write a series of travel articles eight weeks after

Izzy was born. Barely had I finished my laundry from that trip than I was away to Miami, watching its Cuban population react to the death of Fidel Castro. Australia followed – two months of jetting back and forth across the vast continent – and then a return to the United States that ended up covering the best part of a year.

The more I travelled, the more I seemed to be uncovering a version of myself I hadn't even known existed. At the most fundamental level, my ability to keep myself alive in another country was a continuing source of wonder. It was probably a surprise to my parents and my sister too. How was it that I was able to cross 1,200 miles of Australian outback without incident but dinged the car as soon as I was back in Luton? How had I seamlessly navigated Tokyo's intimidating subway system when I couldn't usually negotiate the opening of a packet of coffee without spilling it all over myself?

These hitherto-unknown levels of competence, of organizational and logistical flair, were not the only treasures this other Emma had to offer. Travel Emma was more open and less judgemental; she was a better listener and learned more quickly from her mistakes. She was also, crucially, unencumbered by what her friends and family already knew her to be. There was no need to make a joke of her clumsiness or apologize for her inability to find a boyfriend because the people she met didn't see her as

hopelessly clumsy or tragically single. They saw her as something else: someone intrepid, resilient and confident.

In Japan I met a pair of friends, Jacqui and Susan. They were on the group walking tour I'd been sent to write about and we bonded over pungent breakfasts of fermented soybeans, stiff walks up steep mountains and evenings in onsens, where we bathed our aching calves and butts in the hot spa waters.

Friendships made on the road might have been quick-drying but they were rarely superficial – if anything the opposite. Being cut off from the familiarity and safety of home, and reliant on the goodwill of others, demanded a surprising trust and intimacy with people I barely knew. Plus, it was hard to be standoffish with anyone when you were compulsorily naked together every day.

Both women were a good 30 years older than me and I was fascinated by the tale of their friendship formed in college when they were firebrand activists ready to take on the world in the summer of '68. Jacqui started an arts charity; Susan went into marketing. They both married, and had kids, and divorced; they both experienced the ache of empty nest syndrome and the restorative joy of becoming grandparents. They hadn't seen each other for the decades that they lived in different states. Then they reconnected and this was the third trip they had been on together in a year.

They asked to hear my own story and I explained that there was nothing to tell. I wasn't married, didn't have kids or even a job right now. I was drifting; I'd have to find something more stable, eventually, to help pay the mortgage, but staff jobs at newspapers were hard to come by and I was unlikely ever to find another. 'Perhaps this is early retirement,' I joked. 'Perhaps I'm just taking it in the middle of my career instead of near the end.'

'But you enjoy the travelling,' said Jacqui.

'Definitely,' I said. 'I get to meet great people like you.'

'Well, couldn't that be your future? What's to stop you doing this forever?'

Jacqui had a point. It was true that I was free of all ties, commitments, dependants. No one at home needed me and travelling had proved that I could get by just fine on my own. But the sudden escape to an alternate reality didn't come without a twist of guilt. Heather was still recovering from cancer – successfully, yet it didn't feel like the act of a best friend to keep disappearing the way I was. She shrugged and said that everyone had to earn a living. She also said she missed me. I sent her daily updates wherever I was in the world but learned to hold back the gratuitous details of my cushiest jobs, like the week-long cruise around a succession of Caribbean islands.

As for my newly minted aunthood, I tried to balance my long absences with periods of hyperactive helpfulness

whenever I returned home. Mum noted, with some surprise, my continuing willingness to overnight in my sister's spare bedroom. 'But it's right next to the baby's room,' she said. 'Don't you get woken up whenever she cries?' I told her that all the long-haul flights were good training and that I owned a powerfully effective set of earplugs. Both things were true but another truth was that I didn't really mind being woken up. It was worth it to feel part of the effort, part of the team.

Whether my stays were more trouble than they were worth remained arguable, though. The baby quite understandably forgot me between visits and the sudden presence of someone who looked so like, yet wasn't, her mother would send her into a state of alarm for at least 24 hours. The ensuing clinginess generally meant that Kate couldn't even hand her off to nip into the bathroom without triggering a meltdown. Attempts to tag me in at dinner or bathtime were met with howls of rage. As a substitute parent, it was difficult to get off the bench.

My most effective role became as a late-night babysitter who hid in the wings until Kate or Justin had bathed Izzy and got her down for the night. This did, at least, give them the chance to escape the house for an evening, while I drank the beer in their fridge and ate the pizza they'd ordered for me. It did nothing to shake the impression that I was still somehow an overage teenager, that my current

globetrotting was merely a belated gap year, an indication that, unlike my peers, I had never managed to find myself a grown-up life.

Travel Emma would vanish immediately on passing customs. My parents' house was a shortish drive from Heathrow airport and often one or other of them would volunteer to pick me up from whatever red-eye flight had landed me back in its bleached neon lighting, to the smell of a Costa coffee and a soggy croque monsieur. 'How was the trip?' they'd ask, and I'd talk about the hold-up on the tarmac or the turbulence over the mid-Atlantic while the vivid visions of foreign landscapes and the intense friendships I'd made with people I would never see again faded into the recesses of my mind and took on the quality of a private dream.

Some stubborn part of me knew that I would never be able to share the experiences satisfyingly enough and refused to even try. Maybe it was a protective measure, too; I didn't want to reduce everything I'd been through to some kind of show and tell. I once tried to explain some of the more profound changes I'd felt in myself to Justin, who had always loved travelling in the States. 'You might want to tone it down a bit,' he said. 'You sound like you've joined a cult.'

It was simpler to accept that my two lives didn't translate on to each other. Instead, when I was home,

I let the other world go and focused myself on the limited time period that existed to be a daughter, a sister and an aunt. Grand road trips across vast tracts of wilderness were replaced with afternoon excursions to Hitchin and Milton Keynes – a walk round the shops, lunch at a Pizza Express – and instead of being the one at the wheel, I surrendered myself to life in the back seat of my parents' Mini or Kate's Toyota Auris.

Up front, the adults carried on their conversations about the household insurance premium or where best to park. I kept Izzy entertained in her car seat, pulling faces to distract her from the fact she was hungry, or tired, or whatever it was making her bottom lip wobble. The jester role had its rewards – like the satisfaction of making her laugh – but just occasionally I felt it chafing, as if I was being squeezed into a tight-fitting costume that someone else had chosen for me. On those occasions, anxiety would grip me – a sudden dismay that the view from the back seat was all there would ever be for me, here at home.

I was on assignment in the US when Izzy celebrated her first birthday, staying with Susan, the woman I'd met in Japan, who had offered to put me up in her comfortable condo. Most of my niece's early milestones had been distantly marked via deadpan texts ('She stood up, fell over and nutted the carpet') and video clips on WhatsApp.

Receiving them, I would suddenly miss her dreadfully, even if I hadn't thought of her for days, even though she was just a baby who mostly cried when I was around her.

It was disturbing, the pull I could feel just from a few pictures. Izzy's quiff of curly hair grew only on the top of her head, giving her a mini-Mohican and leading most casual observers to mistake her for a boy. Her oversize eyes were, I knew, just an evolutionary development to make sure that humans looked after their offspring rather than ate them. The complex expressions I read into her features – pity, irony, contempt – could only be a trick of the camera. And yet, those images jangled my own emotions like puppet-strings.

I felt guilty about being out of the country for her first ever birthday but my sister assured me I wasn't missing anything. 'It's not like we'll be playing party games with a baby, is it? She won't even remember it.'

Still, Kate had baked a Nemo-shaped cake and devoted most of the weekend to decorating it, and I joined in the family gathering that was taking place 4,000 miles away via video call. At least, I tried to. The call connected to a quick-panning close-up of the dining room floor, while my mother, an unwitting voiceover artist, provided the narration.

'She's just dropped a bit of it on the carpet, let me pick it up . . .'

'Don't worry about that Christine, I'll get it.'

'No, no, I've got a cloth now – here, someone take the phone . . .'

A noisy scuffling followed and the screen swayed nauseatingly until it finally settled itself upright. My father's face loomed into view.

'Oh, it's you,' he said. 'Sorry, it's a bit busy here.'

'I can hear that.' The background of loud yet indistinguishable conversations made me irritable. 'Sounds like you're having a good party.'

'Yes, very good.'

There was a long pause. My dad had never been good at phone conversations.

'Can I see the cake?'

'We've already eaten that, it was delicious.'

'Well, show me the birthday girl then.'

The screen flipped to reveal Kate's living room crowded with relatives. Isabella was nestled in the lap of her other aunt, Justin's sister. I felt a jealous pang.

'Shall I hand you to Kate?' Dad was saying. 'Oh, wait, she's just heading to the kitchen . . .' He seemed keen to palm me off. 'Here, I'll prop you up on the sofa and you can see what's going on.'

'Don't worry, it's too noisy to hear much. I'll call back later.'

'All right then.'

'Say hi to everyone for me.'

'Will do.'

I left the virtual party and returned to the real world a little sore. Sitting on Susan's sofa, feeling exiled from family life, the conversation we'd had in Japan came back to me, and Jacqui's question: 'What's to stop you doing this forever?' I asked my older, wiser friend why everything always had to be either/or and why neither option was entirely satisfying. 'Probably because you're a woman,' shrugged Susan. 'I don't think we can escape it. We feel these things in our bones.'

I recalled the feeling I had whenever Izzy was asleep on my chest, the physical thread that seemed to attach between us. I thought of how, even though I hadn't been responsible for her, I felt peculiarly responsible for her. I wondered if that was to do with DNA or dopamine, biology or gender, or whether the explanation went beyond what science could offer.

Either way, it was clearly inescapable. The idea of an entirely untethered existence was impossible. However self-sufficient I was proving myself to be, however exhilarated by my flair for making connections, however happy in my independence, my extraordinary freedom was being over-ridden by a stronger impulse.

I tried to shake it by imagining a life on the road with its constant promise of being my own better half. Always in

the driving seat, never confined to the back: it should have been my dream. Instead, I knew with a sudden certainty that it wasn't something I wanted. Travelling may have loosened plenty of bonds but it had also revealed the ones that mattered.

It reminded me of a haunted house attraction that my sister and I once went to in the full knowledge that it would scare the bejesus out of us. We had gripped each other's hands as we'd entered and clung to each other's arms as we made our way around; by the time we were two-thirds through we were shuffling forward as if we shared a single torso. And then, just before the final room, we'd been funnelled through a cattle crush that had separated us, sending each of us down a different corridor, black and unlit. The horror at realizing we were being separated was excruciating – worse, as it turned out, than anything else that awaited us. We threw ourselves down those dark corridors in a frenzy of fear and burst from the exit into a well-lit street. And when we fell into each other's arms, shaking with relief, we said we'd never had so much fun in our lives.

CHAPTER 11

Women's brains supposedly encourage them to forget the excruciating pain of childbirth. Perched uncomfortably at the edge of a dancefloor, attempting to hold myself up against the jostle of passing bodies, I realized that they do the same with high heels.

It had been a while since I had last spent a night with my size nines perched on top of a pair of miniature ski slopes, nothing but a couple of narrow straps of fabric and the combined efforts of every one of my muscle groups preventing them from sliding off. But I recognized it well – the razor-sharp pinching of my toes, the nascent laceration behind my heels, the sensation that someone was operating a pile driver through the balls of my feet, and that someone was me.

My mind went back to the moment I'd stood in front of my wardrobe, held this very pair of gold-sprayed strappy sandals in my hand and told the anxious voice in my head that we'd be *fine*. That *these ones* didn't hurt that bad. Now I foresaw that by the time this night was over the skin on my right little toe would be shredded, adding a deeper patch of russet brown to the inside of the leather, and my left heel would have worked up a blister so large that I'd be unable to walk without wincing for days to come.

Still, there was nothing I could do about it now. My cruel ego had known that when it fooled me into packing these ridiculous shoes. Instead I focused my physical efforts on moving my weary legs side to side in time to the beat and masking the wince each time I transferred my weight. It felt like I was performing the world's smallest, but cruellest, bleep test.

I wished I was drunk, or at least tipsier than I was. But the G&Ts here cost 15 quid and the only buzz I could afford was the quiver of indignation at the prices. The club had been chosen — like everything else today — by Ally's politburo of bridesmaids, who had picked it because they considered it 'just trashy enough' for the occasion. Towards the centre of the heaving dancefloor two of them were practising their slut drops while the bride-to-be shimmied her shoulders in a more conservative style.

A woman bopping along next to me leaned over and garbled something into my ear with an excited energy that suggested she'd had some kind of religious epiphany. I had no idea what she was saying but I nodded and laughed and tried to match her expression with something similarly ecstatic. Was this one called Kelly, or Caitlin, or something like that? I couldn't remember. It didn't really matter, not here, trapped inside the all-obliterating aural onslaught of disco cheese. And possibly never, if I could avoid conversation with her for the rest of the weekend.

I resisted the urge to look at my watch. It was probably only a quarter of an hour since the last time I'd snuck a glance and I had no idea how much longer we were expected to stay here pretending to have the times of our lives.

She might have been one of the Sarahs.

Ally had told me, when we were both disparaging hen-dos in the past, that she definitely, definitely didn't want one – or at least, not a traditional one, not one with just women and not one that involved her wearing a veil or an L-plate or penis-shaped earrings. The fact she was wearing all three right now was allegedly ironic. This was, after all, merely the 'cheesy' portion of what her Co-Chief Bridesmaid (Logistics) had described as a 'modular' weekend meant to 'celebrate our amazing girl in the style she deserves'.

There were hints, in the original email chain, that the style that Ally's other girlfriends were referring to was one I might struggle to afford: for instance, the £150 deposit we were each required to transfer for the cooking class-and-manicure section of the weekend. On meeting them that morning, in the Cotswolds village where they had grown up together, the hints had become klaxons.

A group of immaculately attired women, most of whom had known Ally from her schooldays, smiled at me graciously when we were introduced, before returning to a conversation about a sailing trip they'd all been on

and complimenting each other's most recent handbag purchases. I focused instead on feeding a sticky pile of floury mess into an expensive pasta machine. Someone noticed my struggle and asked if I'd never owned one before.

Over the course of the day, I wondered how on earth it was possible that these women and I had anything in common, let alone a good friend. The Co-Chief Bridesmaid (Entertainment) had allotted, within our sprawling schedule, some afternoon relaxation time around her full-length swimming pool. Most of the girls shared gossip about their friends, and their friends' more famous siblings. The few of us who hadn't grown up around wealth asked each other what jobs we did and how long we'd known Ally, until even those conversations sputtered out into awkward silences.

It was nearly 9pm before we left the house for dinner and dancing. Our departure followed an interminable early evening spent 'getting ready', an activity which had been assigned a couple of hours in its own right and explained why so many of the women had brought cabin-sized wheelie suitcases for a single-night stay. I usually lost interest in blow-drying my hair after five minutes or as soon as my arm got tired and I felt queasy at the thought of spending an hour in front of a mirror with a pair of curling tongs, a sort of anti-motion sickness. My pencil case-

sized make-up bag inspired one of Ally's schoolfriends to actually speak to me. 'Wow,' she said, as she glanced at the sticks of mascara and lippy within. 'I wish I could pack that light.'

And now we were in the club and I should have been trying to enjoy myself but, even aside from the stabbing pain in my feet, it was hard, when I was this sober, to remember how to dance without feeling self-conscious. Instead, my limbs jagged about, too tired to coordinate, my stomach muscles ached from holding me up on these stupid stilts and my whole mind was preoccupied in a blur of agony, impatience and flight instinct. I looked at Ally in the middle of the floor, surrounded by a group of women nailing all the moves to 'Saturday Night', and I reminded myself there was a reason I never did do girls' nights out.

To be fair, I didn't do girls' nights in, either.

In fact I had, throughout my adult life, tended to avoid anything that presented itself as an all-female gathering. Just the idea made me want to run in the opposite direction. I told myself it was an aversion to cliché, an irritation with the message that, as a single woman, I was 'supposed' to enjoy this kind of socializing and bonding exercise. After all, according to American TV shows and early 21st-century marketeers, if I didn't have a family of my own then my next best option was a gang of gal pals with whom I could regularly drain a half-dozen bottles of wine on a

Saturday night. Usually while sitting on a large sofa in a neutral shade of oatmeal and laughing off my disastrous sexual encounters with (multiple) men.

Why was I so intolerant? Having a band of female friends wasn't a harmful or demeaning notion; it didn't threaten to hold me back or marginalize me. It was, in fact, a perfectly life-affirming concept (at least what I saw of it on the Jacob's Creek adverts). And yet you could present it in as cosy and benign way as you liked and my lip still auto-curled with contempt. I couldn't avoid the sense that not only was I nothing like these women who giggled over their rosé and cried over their feelings but that I didn't much want to be like them either.

Perhaps it isn't a surprise that someone who spent 15 years in all-girls' schools should develop an allergy to single-sex gatherings. Perhaps I was pushing back at the idea that society was trying to tell me which interactions were most empowering for me. Either way, any invitation appended with the words 'just the girls' pretty much guaranteed my non-attendance. At college, the idea that my female peers wanted to waste their time in what sounded like self-imposed confinement had truly baffled me. What was the point of talking *about* men when it was so much more interesting to talk *to* them?

For a while I was convinced that this particular female rite was nothing but an emperor's-new-clothes bid to

appear grown-up and sophisticated, an aspirational nod to Carrie Bradshaw and her crew, created and sustained by the pernicious lobbying influence of Big Wine. Then, as adulthood progressed, it became clear that my female friends were finding genuine solace and spiritual uplift when they got together without the guys. *I* was the outlier, the one whose sense of reality was askew. Evidently, it wasn't just the motherhood instinct I was lacking. I was inclined to let down the sisterhood as well.

There might be half a dozen women gathered, all delightful people worthy of my attention; maybe one of them had even cooked the rest of us a delicious meal. Someone would be sharing the story of their day, or their week, or their life. The others, with a patience and a kindness I couldn't match, would be picking up on mundane details and asking tender questions.

'And is there any way you can tell your boss how you feel?'

Often I would suddenly come to halfway through one of these stories and realize I'd been paying absolutely no attention to what it was about or whose side I was supposed to be on. By the time the invisible talking baton reached me I would be desperate to turn the talk to something more trivial. 'And how are you doing, Emma?' 'Great, thanks! I've got *really* into *Justified* . . .'

Group lament frustrated me; it felt bootless, fruitless

and oddly tribal, a sort of staged retreat behind gender lines. Often the process transformed a relatively simple issue into something far heavier or more complicated than it needed to be. For instance, if a guy wasn't responding to someone's text messages, it was fair to infer that he probably wasn't all that bothered about the person sending them.

It was rare, however, to see this unpalatable truth confronted head on. Instead, the text messages would need to be read aloud, discussed and analysed as if they were some kind of cypher, and then the group would spin a fantasy list of reasons the guy in question might not be responding, along with an infinite set of things he might be – and yet almost certainly wasn't – thinking.

I got that there were times when men *were* from Mars. But making an appointment to bemoan this fact felt more than a little self-perpetuating – even a kind of celebration of failure. There was something uncomfortably self-effacing in getting together with other women to bemoan one's singleness. It was true that my best efforts hadn't changed the fact I was single. But I was still reticent to treat it as some kind of disease that desperately needed curing.

Marisa, understanding friend that she was, had never pressed me into her own girl gang. But she never counted me out either. 'I know it's not your thing,' she would begin,

before telling me of some hangout that was happening soon and reminding me I was always welcome. Several of Marisa's closest friends moved on and out of town while she was living in New Zealand and when she returned to London, 18 months later, she made a point of getting to know mine. The implication that I had good taste in mates was flattering and she bonded quickly with the girls. When I went off on my own travels, they had, together, rallied around Heather, making sure she had the support she needed.

Plenty else happened while I was away. Heather moved into her own place, in the same neighbourhood as my flat; Nicola married the man she'd been dating for the past couple of years and they bought a place nearby. Marisa, meanwhile, met a guy called Luke. They got engaged, an event we celebrated together on opposite sides of the Atlantic Ocean via WhatsApp. It made me happy to know, even from a distance, that the ladies I cared about were doing so well.

By the time my two years of peripatetic living were up and I moved back into my flat, a little community had sprung up. On Fridays there was a floating film-and-pizza night that drew in Neil and Bledi and various others who lived in the same locale. On Wednesdays, the girls got together alone to ponder big questions and engage in some kind of self-improvement course.

'I know it's not your thing,' said Marisa when I got home, 'but you might enjoy it. And I don't want you to feel like I've hijacked your mates. We've all really missed you, you know.' I told her not to be silly; I was chuffed that I'd landed back home to an instant community and that I was going to see plenty of everyone now that they were living so close by. But I said thanks but no thanks to the Wednesday introspection.

There was one more reason I felt resistant. While I was away, I had turned 40. Travel Emma, ensconced in her adventurous alternate reality, had breezed past this milestone, barely glancing out of the window at its blurry edges. Age meant little on the road, where the world felt like an infinite web of possibility and connection. But now, as I plugged back into the matrix of friends and colleagues, of comparative career paths and other people's houses, my difference felt more like failure. It might have been illogical but here in London, the city of opportunity, my options seemed more limited and my future less hopeful.

For the first time, it didn't help that so many of my friends were younger than me. Mine was now, officially, the most extreme case of singleness that I knew of. I was a solitary scout – the first of my tribe to survey the bleak uplands of a fifth decade without ever having had a partner. And no matter how hard I tried to forget it, that big round number just kept presenting itself – mostly when someone

asked my age and I thought, for half a second, about lying.

Forty felt like the point of no return, since from now on, even men in their thirties would consider me old. While I had never previously considered myself a *massive* catch – I would probably have rated myself a seven on personality, a six on looks – there had always been a certain youthful energy on my side. In my mid-thirties, when people discovered my age they often expressed surprise – I didn't look it! They'd have put me in my twenties! – and I had ridden that wave for all it was worth, secretly smug to claim the best of both worlds, the looks of a younger woman with the urbane knowledge of an older one.

Now, when I was forced to admit I was 40, no one told me I didn't look it. They just nodded politely. This made no sense to me – I was the same size and shape with the same facial features. My grey roots were dyed the moment they peeped through. What had changed? It wasn't as if I'd taken up smoking or become prime minister; my moisturizing regime was impeccable and I saw no incipient wrinkles in the mirror. Yet people were happy to accept that I was a 40-year-old woman. Whereas I was not.

Phrases that had never before applied to me – on the shelf, undesirable, old maid – now tumbled out of the air and into my brain as I tried to sleep, burying me in an avalanche of self-pity. Tightly cloaked in my own insecurities, I had to tamp down my irritation over other

people's complaints – other women's, especially. I was increasingly disinclined to be generous; at times my sympathy simply ran dry. A young friend I hadn't seen in a long while invited me round for tea and talked about her struggle to get pregnant. She was upset and I hated to see that but fertility issues had always been an emotional blind spot for me. The inability to have a baby was a pain I could neither conjure nor understand and, to be brutally honest, I had never much tried.

But I listened patiently and adopted a caring expression. It just felt so unfair, she said. It had been hard enough to find someone to fall in love with. Couldn't just one part of the process have been easy? As I nodded and murmured comfort, I mentally added up how much time she'd spent on a dating website before she met her husband and how long she'd been trying for a baby. It didn't come to much more than a year. My carefully controlled jawline felt like it was about to crack and fall away from my face. My skin seemed to harden to a crust.

I worried, sometimes, that my lack of empathy made me a monster. If I wasn't going to be the princess in my own story, I clearly wasn't going to be someone else's fairy godmother. More likely I was the cautionary part of the tale: the witch, perhaps, eaten up by bitterness at a world that didn't appreciate her. After all, what really was the point in all this heavy-duty emotional investment in friends

who were always going to move on and leave you behind? At some stage, I was going to run out of people who I had a life in common with. And then I'd be entirely alone.

Not yet, however. There were other single women in our little local community: Joanna, Robin, Cassie and Tessa. Tessa was part of the Wednesday night set-up that I didn't go to and the Friday film night that I did. She was training for the priesthood and had a habit of cocking her head a little to one side as she listened to you – exactly the kind of mannerism I imagined that a vicar should have. Her earnestness intimidated me. You'd be telling a story, one that you were sure was going to elicit a big laugh, and at the climax she'd issue a contemplative hum and ask some unnerving question, for instance: 'And was that the outcome you intended?'

Tessa wasn't the kind of woman I pictured myself being close to. She seemed like a person who thought about things more deeply and took them far more to heart than I was prepared to. She wasn't unremittingly serious: when I first met her, on that group holiday with Aggie, she had been the originator of kitchen karaoke, belting out 'Eternal Flame' into a slotted spoon. But other times she absorbed what was going on around her so quietly that I couldn't tell whether she was actually enjoying herself or sitting in quiet judgement.

And then another holiday friend, Naomi, split up

with her boyfriend and Tessa and Nicola suggested that we take her to the pub and console her. Since this was an emergency mission, it was exempt from my usual protocol against all-female hangouts. We couldn't exactly invite the guys along, since one of them was the ex-boyfriend. And anyway, I was happy to be on the welcoming committee for a woman returning to the single fold. If there was one aspect of other people's relationships that was never boring, it was the break up; it was also the feature I was most able to relate to.

This particular evening turned out to be more fun than any of us expected, not least the heartbreak victim. There was no whining or wallowing, although Tessa did express some mordant thoughts on the arrested development of her male peers, in language far swearier than you'd expect from a future woman-of-the-cloth. Mostly, we avoided the topic of men entirely – we talked about our favourite curry houses and Nicola's bizarre obsession with Celine Dion; we discussed whether invisible braces worked and whether anyone ever noticed how straight your teeth were anyway.

And at the end of the evening, when everyone agreed we'd had a good time, the girls proposed we do it again in a few weeks. It was only when the date was going into our calendars that I had second thoughts. What if we couldn't repeat the chemistry? What if we ran out of funny things

to discuss and were forced to talk about our feelings instead? Nicola suggested we meet at her place for dinner; her husband would disappear upstairs, she said, and she'd bake us all a pie. A *pie*? I felt a shiver of unease.

It sounded like a pastry-crusted trap.

Once again, I was proven wrong. Over dinner, I started telling the girls about a pickle I had got myself into during the week when I was putting things away in my loft. I had accidentally kicked over the stepladder as I tried to lower myself back down through the hatch and was suspended there for a moment, a pair of cartoon legs bicycling in mid-air, before I managed to haul myself back up. Tessa sniggered loudly. It was the least ladylike sound I'd ever heard her make.

I resumed the tale: how I'd spent the next five minutes looking regretfully at the phone that languished on the bed below me and a full quarter-hour perched uncomfortably on the wooden slats around the opening, breathing in insulation particles and wondering how on earth I was going to get down without breaking any bones. It was, quite possibly, the longest period of pure reflection I had ever managed. Over that time I mapped out a number of possible futures, in which I:

(a) simply remained in the loft until my skeleton was found,

(b) lowered myself by my arms using the surfeit of bicep power I never knew I had, or

(c) attempted to dive headfirst onto my bed at an acute angle that might just break my neck.

Eventually, realizing I'd already reached my *127 Hours* moment and that I would probably die of boredom before starvation, I found a combination of (b) and (c) that landed me heavily on the floor – but only after I'd bounced off the edge of the mattress and thus broken the worst of my fall.

I was regretting, to my audience, that I didn't even have any decent bruises to show them for my extreme bravery, when I noticed that Tessa's entire body was shaking as if racked with sobs. The other three of us stared as she silently convulsed and the more we watched her ineffective efforts to control herself, the funnier they became. Soon the hysteria had infected us all and not one of us could speak for laughing; even as I cycled home that night, I only had to think of it to trigger another bout that nearly knocked me off my bike.

When was the last time I had belly laughed like that? I couldn't have told you but I knew I wanted a repeat. And so each time another of these little gatherings was mooted, I was there, until the night we all agreed to meet for a meal out and I got a last-minute text from a guy I had a massive crush on.

His name was Ash and I had fancied him the moment I met him, a couple of months previously. Since then we had met up three times, always with work-related pretexts, but we got on encouragingly well and, more importantly, had established exactly the kind of regular friendly text banter that, while innocent, could certainly have counted as flirtation. Now he was texting to say he had spent the day working in my part of town. Did I fancy a drink nearby? I was a heterosexual single woman and he was a man who was as handsome as he was smart and charming. So yes, yes, yes, I did very much want to meet for a drink. I texted the girls and told them what had happened and that I would let them know if I was going to be late for dinner.

Travelling, while a fillip for my soul, had failed to stoke my sputtering romantic prospects. How it was that I was able to meet so many interesting new people and for almost every single one of them to be happily partnered was either a cruel joke on the part of the universe or a statistical quirk of 21st-century demography, depending on how I was feeling when I thought about it.

You could argue that I still had a love life. For instance, I regularly fell in love with characters from my favourite boxsets (and sometimes, if they put in a good performance on *Graham Norton*, with the actors playing them). I even had a type: I tended to fall for supporting characters, for the everymen, for loser-ish underdogs. Once I daydreamed a

multi-arc piece of *Justified* fan-fiction in which I formed an alliance with a minor character who never got enough screen time for my liking. (I didn't have the imagination for some kinky E L James storyline – we just drove round the Appalachians busting crimes and having laconic conversation girded with sexual tension.)

Kate and Justin both regularly expressed their bafflement at the guys I found attractive but I thought that was a good sign: it wasn't as if my fantasy men were out of my league or I was expecting to snag the handsome lead. And anyway, I wasn't completely tragic – I fancied real people too. Usually they were men in some industry that interconnected with mine, who I met briefly in person or had some dealing with over email, and whose existence in the world brought a flutter of excitement to my life, right up until I discovered they were married or about to move into a Peruvian monastery.

Sometimes I encountered them on social media, where they were pithily witty and wore a gilet in their profile pic to suggest they were equally at home in the city or the countryside. Twitter infatuations were especially emotional rides: a flurry of one-upping one-liners, followed by some back-and-forth DMs, while I scoured their bio, then their website, then Google images, and began mentally constructing the painstaking path to our transatlantic life together (they often lived in another

country). I was usually besotted by the time I came across the picture with their arm round their extremely hot girlfriend. Neutral to heartbreak in under 300 seconds.

In this context, being asked to meet up by an actual three-dimensional human being – one who had been regularly messaging and told me, with his own lips, that he was single – was kind of a big deal. Scratch that, it was the biggest deal, the most hopeful thing that had occurred on the man front in well over a year. (Someone should make a porn-film-noir called 'On the Man Front', incidentally, starring a Marlon Brando lookalike. I'd watch it.)

It was hard to gauge Ash's age exactly. He had no grey hairs that I could see. His physique suggested one of those people who kept themselves in shape by running every day, and there was something in his manner, too, suggesting he considered himself in the prime of life. From little clues in his speech, however – the pop culture he referenced, the fact he remembered parts of the seventies – I knew he must be quite a few years older than me. That realization was strangely heartening. When I'd been online dating, I had become discouraged by how rapidly many men seemed to age past their 40s, and worried that I might be sailing towards some kind of event horizon, beyond which I would never find anyone my own age attractive again.

Also, being younger than him was surely in my favour. Even I could be a catch for an older man.

In the pub, we sat drinking pints and talking on subjects we both enjoyed while my rusty antennae tried to scan for signals. Ash seemed to be genuinely enjoying my company – talking enthusiastically, going to the bar to buy us more drinks as soon as he'd finished his first. On the other hand, he seemed to have left a more-than-courteous amount of space between us in the semicircular booth in which we were sitting. It was impossible to swat his arm flirtatiously while laughing at his jokes – the only move I had ever learned – when he was that far away. Not without looking like I was planning to assault him.

So instead I kept drinking and encouraged him to talk about himself. I suggested a third pint, clinging to our interaction with tenacious optimism, and the more we sat and talked, the more I felt I had in common with this attractive man who was, after all, still single like me. Time dilated, as is its wont, somewhere between drinks three and five. A foggy voice in my head, transmitted down an increasingly unclear line, reminded me that I needed to contact the girls. But I couldn't exactly text them under the table, not when I was working this hard to maintain eye contact.

Eventually, I managed to excuse myself to the bathroom and message them: *Sorry ladies, not going to make it. Things are going well, got to see it through!* They would understand; this was for the greater good of womanity,

after all. And they would be triumphantly complicit in any future marriage.

I put my phone away and concentrated on my date, and on not sounding too drunk. An hour later, I sensed the silent application of brakes, a rumbling deceleration as the evening approached its final stop. Our glasses had nearly run dry; so had my companion's enthusiasm. We stood up and gathered our coats and walked out to the road; Ash gave me a hug that contained not a hint of a linger. He checked that I was OK to walk home alone and ordered himself an Uber. That was it. It wasn't so much that I had misread the signs as hallucinated them.

Silently gurgling with shame and disappointment, I reached into my pocket and pulled out my phone, scrolling as I walked. A big red button alerted me to a number of WhatsApp messages from the girls. I opened them. And instantly realized I was in trouble.

What the what? You're ditching us for a guy???

Gonna be honest, didn't think you were that person . . .

Not cool, EJ. Not cool.

I tried to respond with a touch of levity. If it made them feel better, I said, the 'date' had been a bust; I truly regretted my actions (I didn't) and hanging out in their company would have made for a far more satisfying evening. Surely the tale of thwarted romantic ambition would win me some sympathy? But there was only cooling radio silence.

The walk home was a painfully dejected one. I wasn't sure whether I felt more aggrieved at the girls or at Ash – or, indeed, at myself, for having let my hopes inflate so recklessly fast. Looking back over the evening, I tried to be objective, but all I could remember was how animated our conversation had been. I thought back over the messages, too, and the burgeoning chemistry of the past few weeks that I now supposed I must have imagined. Or perhaps, initially, I had offered a glimpse of girlfriend potential, and I wondered in what regards I had failed the test – whether it was looks, or my manner, or something even more innate.

Ash's casual self-assurance – one of his undeniably attractive qualities – made my own confidence seem insubstantial by comparison, something assumed rather than organic. How were single guys older than me able to be so sure of themselves, so certain of their appeal? My mind tallied all the men I knew who had divorced at or even past middle age, and instantly started dating women – attractive, impressive women – ten or even twenty years younger than them. It sounded like a cliché, and yet I could easily count them into double figures; several of those had married again within the year.

My mind boggled at it, the speed with which my male contemporaries found companionship, the ease with which they surfed down the age ranges. Meanwhile I obfuscated and equivocated when asked questions that might give

away my age, convinced that the moment a man did the maths and realized I was 40, I would have all the appeal of an out-of-date yoghurt. I didn't want to be laughed at, either, as someone who chased impossibly younger men. The last time I had admitted being attracted to someone in their (late) twenties, a male friend had called me a cougar; I'd felt sick with embarrassment and determined never to make that mistake again.

It was the kind of thing I wished I could talk to the girls about, although I knew there would have to be a rapprochement first. After a week of feeling awkward, I received an invitation to dinner at Tessa's. Of the three, she had sounded the most scandalized by my no-show, so I anticipated this would be some kind of reckoning. When it came to confrontation I was a coward and usually the first to back down in any disagreement. But now the thought made me bristle defensively. It still didn't seem to me that I had done anything that wrong.

I turned up at Tessa's house with a bottle of wine and the packet of garlic bread she'd asked to me pick up on the way. For a little while we skirted the controversial subject, fixing on the details of each other's working days, distracted by the practicalities of assembling a salad. And then the oven timer bleated, the plates were heaped with steaming shepherd's pie and we sat down opposite each other at a small square table that felt like the kind they use in interrogations.

Perhaps it was best to get in first, I thought. 'I'm sorry I stood you guys up last week.' It was technically an apology but delivered in a matter-of-fact tone that strongly implied an absence of regret. The ghost of an unspoken 'but . . .' hovered at the end of the sentence.

'Yeah, what was that about?' said Tessa, holding my gaze from the other side of the table as surely as if she'd pinned me in the face with her fork. 'I'll be honest, I was surprised. It just didn't seem like you.'

'Well, I was surprised that you guys were upset. It's not like I meet men I fancy every day. And never ones who might just *possibly* like me back. I thought you'd all be cheering me on.'

'But we'd made plans. You not bothering to turn up is basically saying to the rest of us that we're not as important as some guy you barely know.'

This was crazy talk: we saw each other all the time. Whereas, I pointed out, that impromptu evening with Ash might never have happened again. 'It felt like it could have been *the* moment, you know? You can't just walk out when you think it might be *the* moment.' And I thought something, too, that I didn't say: if it had been a group of guys I'd flaked on, they wouldn't have made such a fuss.

Tessa sighed but didn't look angry. 'The thing you have to understand is, the times we get together, they're really

special to me. It's the closest I feel to anyone. Don't get me wrong, I love my family and everything, but with you guys I get to be fully myself, the person I really am, in a way I don't back at home, or at work, or anywhere else.'

I swallowed a mouthful of shepherd's pie, and a lump of something else that tasted like guilt.

'And it's taken me a really long time to find that. People I feel totally at peace with. People who get me.'

The female friendships I had flashed before me – with Marisa and Heather, with Tessa, Naomi and Nicola. It had been easy to take them for granted. I'd always viewed them as somehow my right: the standard consolation prize I received as a single woman for missing out on marriage.

When I came home from travelling to a profusion of friendships, I had tapped into them as and when I wanted, without ever considering what might be wanted from me. It was rare I felt any great need to put others first, I knew that. But then, no one was reliant on me, physically or emotionally; I was nobody's first phone call. If the result was an independence that frequently blurred the line with selfishness then how could I be blamed? It wasn't as if *I* was anyone's top priority, either.

'Anyway, I'm probably being over-sensitive about it,' Tessa was saying. 'I feel like because I'm single people don't mind flaking on me and it really pisses me off. They assume that since I don't have a family, I'm totally

flexible and always available. As if my schedule isn't just as full as theirs.'

'I get that,' I said. 'But to be honest, being free to be spontaneous is one of my favourite things about being single.'

'That's because you're you,' Tessa smiled. 'What gets to me is being told that my time isn't as valuable or my life isn't as complex.' Her eyes narrowed. 'Like people saying: "I can't believe someone as great as you is single!" They think they're being encouraging but it just proves that they think having a partner is a measure of your worth. Sometimes I want to turn around and say, "I can't believe someone as great as you feels the need to be married," and see how they like it.'

She had a good point. I thought of all the times I had heard that phrase – and of all the times I'd had to smile, to take it as a compliment, even as I felt my pride withering within me. Why did it feel so embarrassing to have my single status pointed out, if being single was nothing to be ashamed of?

However modern and enlightened the society I lived in, however healthy my ego, whatever self-worth I found in family and friendship, or achievement, or my own character, didn't matter. My failure to find a mate was always just that – a failure. No wonder I hadn't wanted to categorize myself as single. No wonder I had tried to place

myself outside of any particular group. I didn't want to partake of the stigma; I didn't want to encounter or even entertain it.

My notion of being 'pre-married' had been forged as a sort of mental safeguard, one that protected me from shame – the shame of being just another spinster. But it couldn't rid me of it. The ignominy still lay there, smothered by constant activity, buried under layers of optimism and vanity. No matter what I did or said, no matter how content I believed myself to be, there remained, somewhere deep inside, the belief that if I couldn't find a partner there must be something wrong with me. The understanding that my life was, in some measure, less full and less fulfilled than other people's. This was what everyone and everything had taught me.

I thought of Ash and his loose-limbed assurance, and wondered if it was at all the same for him. Or whether men in similar positions to me were able to enjoy their singleness and their freedom, without this self-crippling burden of unfulfilled expectation.

I looked at Tessa, calmly and confidently articulating so many of the things that I refused to admit to myself. And I pictured all the individual single women who saw themselves as a freak, an outlier, a malfunctioning reject.

How many assumed that being single was a path you trod, and a battle you fought, alone?

CHAPTER 12

Dad and I sat next to each other on the sofa, watching a double bill of *M*A*S*H*. We had landed on the programme a few weeks before playing on one of those old rerun channels while we scrolled through the schedule looking for something to watch while we ate our dinner. Finding a TV show that held mutual attraction for us was hard. Dad liked bone-dry documentaries or anything involving engines, machines or gadgets. My Netflix selection of millennial comedies, meanwhile, he found crude and unfunny. Modern drama was cruelly and quite literally booby-trapped with sex scenes, primed to explode in a shower of father–daughter mortification.

Since we never saw Hawkeye make it past first base with any of the nurses, the antics of MASH unit 4077 were now the regular accompaniment to our evening meals. Poignant medical comedy was a peculiar choice, given that we were only here together because Mum was in hospital. On this particular evening, Patrick Swayze had made an unexpected appearance as a soldier who wanted to give blood for his buddy. We were still trying to figure out how young Swayze must have been at the time they filmed it when Hawkeye and Hunnicutt diagnosed him with leukaemia.

I winced and reached for the remote.

'Do we want to watch this?'

Swayze's chiselled cheekbones were struggling with the news of his impending mortality and my skin was prickling with discomfort. Dad shrugged and said it was fine. 'Treatments have come a long way since the Korean war,' he said, his voice halfway to joking. I kept one hand on the control, just in case.

Mum's diagnosis had been just as sudden and unexpected as the Swayze-faced soldier's. She too had seemed robustly healthy before a blood test – ordered after she'd felt out of breath during her usual gym class – returned its results. The GP had called Mum while she was picking up Izzy from preschool and ordered her immediately to hospital; she hadn't left since.

My mother was 66 years old. She was as fit as a flea and inordinately more active; lacking her presence, the house was bizarrely quiet. Usually, the floorboards bristled with the sound of constant movement between the kitchen and the living room. Mum had always found chores where there were none – or at least, none that the rest of us could see. The patch of floor that needed the hoover. The saucepan that wanted bleaching. A piece of gossamer latched to a beam in a far-off corner of the ceiling. Even the laundry basket, squatting out of sight upstairs, seemed to ping out a distress signal that no one but her could hear.

The soundtrack formed by this continual flow of activity – cupboards opening, plates clacking, an iron sizzling – was as eccentric as it was eclectic. It included the background burble of RP voices that emanated tinnily from the back pocket of her jeans from where her phone was broadcasting whatever decades-old radio drama she had found to listen to. On the days when she had exhausted the BBC's output – and such occasions did occur – it was her own external monologue you would hear, punctuating her tasks.

'Well, that's the washing done, what's next?'

Embroidered through the self-commentary were snippets of songs – old music hall numbers she'd learned from her own mother or bits and pieces from ancient pop tunes, their lyrics misremembered or forgotten entirely and substituted with her own ridiculous rhyming schemes. This improvization of nonsense songs was a habit Mum had had since Kate and I were babies. In recent years, with Izzy semi-resident in her house, they had rediscovered their old functions, like stopping an incipient tantrum or coaxing a spoonful of vegetables into a reluctant mouth.

'Here come the peas, here come the peas, everybody know that here come the peas . . .'

Mum was Izzy's unofficial – i.e. unpaid – childminder. Three days a week, my niece was transferred between

identical car seats outside the gates of the zoo where Kate worked. The only time the house fell truly quiet was in the napping hours of the early afternoon when Izzy was cuddled and all-but-hypnotized to sleep with a Pavlovian playlist of soft-core classical string music. During these times, the most desultory attempt at conversation would provoke a fierce glare and a strained shushing, as my father knew well.

Still, Dad's own quietness was comfortably assured. He had spent most of his marriage constructing a place of quiet retreat in his mind and tended, on the whole, to ignore my mother's many audio cues. His selective deafness had recently transmuted, as if in some tale by Aesop or Ovid or Grimm, into actual deafness, a complaint for which he had been issued a state-of-the-art hearing aid, which he never ever wore.

Where Mum liked to announce everything she did – 'I'm just going to make a cup of tea/tidy downstairs/go to the loo' – Dad had the ability to be in a room without speaking for hours or vanish from one entirely without anyone ever noticing. The only time he tended to make his presence felt, in fact, was when any of us was watching a movie. It was then he would throw off his customary reserve in order to better apprise you of each element of the story that could not possibly have happened in real life. There was no anachronism or plot-hole so small that

it was not worthy of Dad's attention – and, by extension, everyone else's.

That trifle aside – and it was only irritating if you wanted to actually watch the movie you were supposed to be watching – Dad's qualities made for an extremely easygoing housemate. He had an outdoor office – a whitewashed, fan-heated shed – to which he would regularly disappear for Skype calls with his friends and, now that he was retired, he kept himself busy all day with various home improvement projects. These, rather than emotional support, were the chief reason that Kate and I had decided that someone should be with him while Mum was in hospital. It wasn't that he wasn't both competent and confident with power tools, but rather that we knew that being alone in the house would make him more ambitious, rather than less. There was a story we often heard from Mum of his determination to fix their washing machine when they were recently married. After she heard a loud thump, she had found him flung against the wall of the utility room, having electrocuted himself with a screwdriver.

We knew we couldn't trust him not to attempt a little light circuitry or suddenly decide that a particular tree in the garden needed felling. If we wanted our mother to survive her illness, we were going to have make sure our father didn't accidentally kill himself in a DIY accident

along the way. (Sure enough, the very afternoon I had arrived back home, a ladder was already leaning against the outside of the house with Dad perched blithely at the top, fixing the roof.)

There was another concern too, this one dietary. Mum had always done the cooking in their house and, on the rare occasions that she was away and Dad was left alone, he tended to turn feral, living off whatever scraps he found in the back of the fridge. Left to himself, he would soon be cutting two-week-old mould from the sides of a block of cheese or arguing that a slight fizz actually improved the taste of hummus.

Even when he did bother to go to a shop, he did so with the scattergun approach of someone who had heard of food but wasn't entirely sure how it worked or how to eat it. He had no more inclination towards the vegetable aisle than the average five year old. The thought of him getting home from the hospital each night to a dinner of miniature pork pies with some microwavable rice made me sad – even if I knew that I had, on occasion, prepared such a meal for myself.

Domestic drama was relatively new to me. I'd had bed bugs in my flat once and, boy, had that felt like the end of the world. Mostly, however, I'd steered a blandly happy course through the ocean of existence and my nuclear family was not the kind you could ever weave a week's

worth of reality TV around. Mum's relations had had a few fallings out in their time but the trouble always seemed remote, like a Scottish weather report.

A couple of years previously, I had mentioned this very fact to my father. We had heard of some sad thing that was happening to some distant cousins on the other side of the world and I had shaken my head and said, with a mixture of foolishness and complacency, that our lives were so easy by comparison and weren't we lucky that we'd never had to face anything terrible at all. And Dad, so much wiser than me, had replied that one day we would but we'd get through it when it happened.

And now here we were, the family stoicism put to the test. The doctors were blunt about Mum's situation. She had a particularly vicious form of leukaemia and, given the state of her blood, they were amazed that she was still alive. Chemotherapy would begin within the week and take several months; as for Mum's future survival, that would depend on a transplant and there was no guarantee of finding one, or of the transplant taking if they did.

When I first joined my parents at the hospital, Mum was sitting on a chair in a common area, waiting to be assigned a room on the haematology ward. I say assigned; Mum was convinced that someone had just died in it and it was now being doused in disinfectant. 'Why else would it be taking so long?' she asked, rhetorically.

She was in peak organizing mode, forcing Dad to make a list of things to bring back on his next trip ('No, Robert, write it *down* or you'll forget'). I sat next to her and held her hand, concentrating hard on the details – she wanted the white earphones, *not* the black ones – to stop myself crying. The familiar sound of her outrageous practicality defeated me. I sank my face into her shoulder and, as she always did at these moments, my mother somehow produced a tissue.

As it happened, the moment of Mum's diagnosis had been so outrageously timed that the week that followed it often felt as comical as it did tragical, which was a blessing of its own. My sister was about to have her second baby and her due date was already positioned dangerously close to the opening of a film festival that my brother-in-law had been working on all year – a four-day event of which he was founder, producer and host.

My sister, on a separate visit, had learned that as soon as the chemo began, Mum's immune system would be too compromised to allow visits from either Izzy or a newborn. Despite her exceptionally brave face, it was clear that Mum found the thought of being separated from them for months – or worse, never getting to hold her new grandchild – the toughest part of her situation. My sister phoned me with a conspiratorial determination. 'So,' she said. 'This baby has to come out of me *now*.'

Since her husband was engaged in one of the busiest weeks of his career, Kate decided not to tell him that she'd called the midwife about hurrying things along. She also decided not to tell him that, on the day the film festival began, the midwife had obliged. Nor did Justin know that the magic of the membrane sweep had worked almost instantly or that while he was making his final on-site preparations for his opening night gala, I was simultaneously driving my sister to the maternity ward.

At reception, Kate tried to warn the nurses of her medical history of shooting out babies at indecent speeds. I tried to reach Justin on the phone. He promised to be there just as soon as he could find someone to take over from him. When he did finally arrive, we were already in the delivery room and my sister was giving me instructions on what to do with Izzy for the rest of the day, holding up her finger at intervals to pause, grimace and suck on gas and air. I tapped out just in time: baby Ethan was born very shortly after I left the room. And Mum spent the weekend before her treatment began cuddling her new grandson.

Within her first week at the hospital, my mother had befriended all the staff on her ward and was on her way to becoming everyone's favourite patient. This despite the fact that she wasn't allowed out of her positive-pressure room with its double-door airlock, since the slightest

infectious sneeze might have killed her. Even with a tree-branch of tubes growing out of her arms, and the skin around them swollen from the fluid, she didn't look remotely sick, only frustrated by her imprisonment. Every morning and afternoon, she got up and walked around for half an hour, pacing the seven or eight steps from the window, round the bed to the door and back again, inspired, she said, by the exercise that Nelson Mandela had taken in his cell on Robben Island. She posted pictures from her window on Facebook and told her friends she was taking 'one day at a time'.

My own instincts were to fall back into the role that I'd found for Heather. I couldn't fix everything – I couldn't, in fact, fix anything – but I could be optimistic, cheerful and thoughtful, and try to make the days as bright as possible. That was the gift that I had to give. And it came with an unexpected sense of purpose, which kept me from internal collapse as surely as a steel insert. Seeing my parents through whatever came next was the only thing I needed to think about or concern myself with. And there was relief in that, and clarity, and a sort of peace.

So I moved back home and Dad and I staggered our visits to the hospital so that Mum had plenty of company. He generally went over in the mornings, taking her a latte from the downstairs cafeteria. I showed up late afternoon, after she'd had a nap. I took in board games that we played

each day, every piece rendered meticulously sterile with an antiseptic wipe (the Scrabble tiles were particularly time-consuming). At 5pm, we had a standing appointment to watch *Pointless* – if I wasn't at the hospital when the programme was on, we called each other and played along over the phone. We took it deadly seriously, sticking to the rules exactly as if we were a team on the show, so that by the time we got to the final round we could fairly claim to have won the trophy ourselves.

I found it hard, initially, to bear the thought of all the hours that Mum was there alone without us; I showered her with books and puzzles to keep her busy until there was no more space on the windowsill for them. But as the days and weeks went on and she got more tired from the treatment, boredom became less of a threat. Sometimes we sat and watched whatever old murder mystery was playing on ITV3, just as we would have done if we'd been home, and she dozed off in the middle, just as she would have if she'd been home. I sat in the armchair next to her bed and held her hand whenever I got the chance because I didn't want to waste any of our time together not holding her hand. And every time we laughed felt golden.

Our new routine brought unexpected benefits. When Mum discovered that there was a gym next to the hospital, she ordered both Dad and I to join it. Soon we were both getting more daily exercise than either of us had bothered

to attempt for a very long time. We were eating well too; I was making a weekly meal-planner, consulting recipe books and actually making dishes with all the right ingredients. My life hadn't felt this well organized since I'd left my office job.

It was also an effective way to stave off internal chaos. Dealing with pain was never my strong suit and my particular emotional coping mechanisms were, I imagined, at least part-derived from my parents. The dominant voice in my head telling me to count my blessings and not to wallow in sad feelings was certainly my mother's; the sudden itchiness to busy myself with practicalities probably came from Dad. The fusion of both into something that psychologists might have termed 'denial' was possibly my own.

If Dad was willing to read up everything the support pamphlets had to say about acute myeloid leukaemia, for instance, that meant I never had to. Unlike Kate, who often called asking for the latest information – a prognosis, a percentage, a cold hard number to brace herself against – I avoided anything that smacked of reality. I could already sense a dark abyss of misery ahead of me and I didn't need anything nudging me further towards it. It was near enough when I closed my eyes at night, a swirling pool of fear and sadness that threatened to suck me down if I didn't fall asleep fast enough.

At home, we talked about how Mum was doing in a comfortingly vague way. Sometimes Dad came home from the hospital saying, 'She's a bit down today,' and it made me realize what a brave face Mum was putting on for me and my sister, and that Dad was trying to carry her sadness as well as his own. Once he stayed late into the evening and when he got home his eyes were wet and he told me he needed a hug. Then he went to the drinks cabinet and poured himself whisky with a heavy hand and a slightly shaky look that I didn't like to see.

But most of the time we kept our emotions private and measured out our love for each other in little acts of kindness. I made fancy dinners. He bought me a book he thought I'd like. We parked Aggie in the middle of the garden and worked on her rusted spots together, touching up the paintwork, reviving her cracked and faded hood with silicone spray. In good weather, we went for walks in the surrounding countryside and we'd amble up a hill in a companionable silence until Dad broke it with a technical observation about the clouds, or to describe a cartoon he'd seen on Facebook, or impart a fact he was clearly desperate to share: 'Do you know about the wombat's deadly bottom?'

We even went on a day trip to London. Before the diagnosis, Mum and Dad had booked tickets to an exhibition of artefacts from Tutankhamun's tomb. They

had celebrated one of their major anniversaries with a cruise along the Nile to see the pyramids, during which they'd both contracted food poisoning and had to spend the entire week in their berths. Egyptology had held an unfinished place in their hearts ever since.

The King Tut tickets were for a specific time and date and couldn't be cancelled, and Mum, stuck in quarantine and shackled to an intravenous infusion machine, thought that Dad and I might at least enjoy them together. So we travelled into town and spent the morning wandering through the dimly lit exhibit, each room rendered black so that the golden treasures shone more spectacularly in their cases. After our daily appointments with beige hospital corridors, their colourful extravagance was a surreal blast to the senses.

We took pictures of our favourite items to show Mum, bought a souvenir catalogue and emerged from the gift shop simultaneously energized and a little shamefaced at the fun we'd had. There was a posh-looking café on the way back to the station and Dad suggested we stop for coffee and cake. The hostess at the door gave us both an indulgent smile; I felt sudden, overwhelming terror that I was about to be mistaken for my father's wife.

This had happened before, more than once, and I was never sure whether to be furiously depressed for my own sake or haughtily disgusted for his. The last time it had happened we were taking Aggie to a car show and the

parking attendant had seen Dad getting out his wallet and joked: 'That's it, make your husband pay!' I'd nearly died in my seat. And still neither of us had corrected him.

Later, after we'd visited Mum and given her the catalogue, Dad retreated to his shed to sort through the slew of paperwork that a health crisis brings. I took him a cup of tea and some biscuits and asked what he was doing. He told me he was trying to cancel the Alaskan trip they had planned for their retirement but it was complicated because each company, from the airline to the hotel to the cruise liner, needed their own proof from the doctors that Mum was actually too sick to travel.

The next day, I baked. This was not something that Mum did, but then it was not something I did, either. I rooted around the backs of her cupboards looking for flour and vanilla essence and gave myself over to the sudden and unaccountable impulse to turn warm, sticky dough into toothsome treats.

The day after, I thought I saw a crumb on the living room carpet. I hoovered just in case.

The doctors who had marvelled that my mother managed to walk into A&E on that first life-or-death day were equally impressed with her handling of chemo. They called her superwoman for the speed with which she recovered from each round. This was somehow no less than I expected of my mother.

It was the fourth round that made her really sick, too ill to see anyone. We tried to Skype but the video calls left her queasy and she just wanted to sleep. Dad still went in to the hospital, to pick up her laundry and bring her a change of clothes. I baked more cakes and made elaborate dinners, and felt guilty as soon as we sat down to eat them. What did I think I was doing, making a five-dish taco feast or buying partridge from the farm shop?

I was now hoovering the living room once a day. I could see why Mum did it now – that carpet *did* show up the dirt. Sometimes I caught myself walking across the living room after my father, my eyes bent downwards, stooping here and there to pick up whatever all but invisible crumbs of dirt had fallen off his shoes. I couldn't leave a room, either, without scanning it for additional pieces of crockery; I barely let Dad finish his cup before I swept it away to the dishwasher.

It was becoming embarrassing, really, how often I caught myself behaving like Mum. I even took up the outrageous feather duster she kept in her bedroom, so vast and plumed it looked like it once fanned Cleopatra, and stuck it into every nook, cranny and corner of the house. After one of these fits of cleaning, I'd throw myself on the sofa with an exhausted sigh and command my father to 'pass me the flicky-dicky', which was Mum's ridiculous word for the remote control. Often Dad ignored me and

I'd realized he hadn't heard what I was saying, and berate him for not wearing his hearing aid. Then I'd settle down to whichever of the antique hunts was taking place on the daytime schedule and find myself unaccountably gripped.

I was, I suppose, trying to keep her place for her, for all of us, willing her to come back. The word 'home' wouldn't have any meaning if she left us.

I missed her terribly. Even when I went in to see her, to take her some clean pyjamas, to say 'hello!' in as bright a voice as I could muster, I missed her. When I thought about the future, and the fact that – maybe next month, maybe next year – I might be alive in a world without her, I missed her so much I thought I might break in half.

I'd spent my whole life trying to prove I was independent of her, annoyed by the influence she exerted over me, rolling my eyes at her keenness to be involved in areas of my life I wanted to keep private and separate from her. But when she was gone, no one would ever care for me in that way again. And I couldn't fathom how to cope with that knowledge or see a way to be happy without her. For an instant, every other relationship in my life felt like it might blow away in the slightest breeze.

It was as if I'd only just noticed how she had been my protector, how I had relied on her for far more than I had ever admitted. I'd taken for granted the things she'd continually given me, like a home I could retreat to when

I was sad or lonely or ill. Like the way she always sent me back to my flat with Tupperware boxes full of leftovers and crisps and biscuits she'd scavenged from her cupboards. My single life had been possible because of her – because she was my safety net, because she was my secret strength. Who would I be without her?

CHAPTER 13

I am staring at my computer screen. Actually, that's not true. If I'm staring at anything, it's a piece of air, about halfway between my screen and my nose. And it's probably more a gaze than a stare. It's hard to stare at vacancy.

Sometimes my glance shifts to the side of the screen and fixes further into the distance, so it might seem, to anyone observing me, that I am looking out of my window, at my garden. In the upper branches of the large horse chestnut tree, parakeets with red collars and beaks perch in surprising numbers. Sometimes they take off and swoop upwards, around and down again, to no apparent purpose. But I'm not really looking at them, either. On other days, the comings and goings in that tree have held me spellbound – the pigeons, parakeets, woodpeckers and daringly gymnastic squirrels – as if they were something out of a children's tale. Today they're just a low-res background, not unlike the one on my laptop.

I don't know how long I've been sitting here, not-staring. It already seems like forever.

A little while ago, I watched a video on my phone. It might have been a minute ago, or five minutes, or half an hour. It was a video of my friend Alex's kitten, Mabel. Mabel was writhing on her back in that state of uninhibited

pleasure that is so enviable to humans, who are forced to behave with more dignity. It probably made me smile, although I can't quite remember now.

Alex has had the kitten since March. She took possession about three days before New York went into lockdown, when people were panic-buying pets. To be fair, Alex has always loved cats and she has always lived alone, so if anyone was going to have one to keep them company during a global pandemic, it seemed only fair that Alex should.

Still, when Alex first walked into the pet shop, a few blocks east of Central Park, the owner told her they were all out. 'They're gone as soon as they come in, honey,' she said. She advised Alex to come back at 11 the next morning when they were expecting their next consignment. Alex arrived at quarter to, just to be sure. The kittens had arrived even earlier and already there was only one remaining – just Mabel, lying in her cage and blinking at the speed of her abandonment. She wasn't called Mabel then, of course.

I don't have any particular affection for cats. If I had a pet, I'd have a dog, and not a silly little lapdog with coiffeured fur or one of those yappy terriers bred with perpetual short-man-syndrome. I would want a proper-sized dog, like a Labrador or a setter or a Dalmatian, the kind of dog too big to lift, the kind you have to get down on the floor to play with or to throw your arms around. But

you can't own a dog like that when you live in an upstairs flat and your nearest park is also a major traffic junction.

Alex has told me she's glad she has Mabel. The kitten has been someone — well, some thing, I suppose — to talk to. Something to fuss over, something to love, something like a naughty child, requiring her near-constant attention. I'm glad Alex has Mabel too. I know that she still gets outside — Alex, that is, not Mabel, who is very much an indoor cat — but it's only to the shop, or to the vast impersonality of Central Park, where everyone else looks like they're going home to someone.

Quite a few of the single women I know have cats. Being a cliché doesn't make it untrue. My friend Joanna has one, as does my friend Genny. Heather doesn't have one but her sourdough starter seems to demand similar amounts of feeding and watering and keeps her plenty occupied. My mate Robin prefers to tend a menagerie of houseplants; her balcony looks like a research station at Kew Gardens. I saw a greetings card once that said 'Plant Lady is the new Cat Lady' and I thought of Robin. And then I thought how insulting the card was.

I suppose, if I've tended to anything during this pandemic, it's been my friendships. The day we got locked down, I wrote a list of all the people I knew who were on their own and put reminders in my calendar to call them every few days. I had so many great phone conversations

that first week, I wondered why I'd never done it before.

One good thing about this locked-down life is that I don't feel much of a freak any more. We're all of us in limbo, everyone on the planet. We're all trapped in aspic — vitals preserved but slowing losing our flavour. Rendered as uninteresting and powerless as jelly.

It's finally OK to be unsexy and unsuccessful because all the actually sexy and successful women in the world are legally prevented from flaunting it outside their houses. It's a strange thing to make me feel better but this year you use what you've got.

Take my parents: a global pandemic has made almost no difference to their lives. When Mum got home from her chemo, she had to stay at home and refuse visits from well-meaning friends. She bulk-bought hand sanitizer and slathered her shopping in anti-bac. Covid was just the rest of the world catching up.

I worry more for Heather. She also had to shield when it all started because of the concerns for anyone with a history of blood cancer and she couldn't even go home to her folks for Christmas because her mum works at a school and it wouldn't have been safe. We meet up for walks in the park and she looks pretty chipper but I know that she's working stupid long hours because there's nothing else to do. I know that she hasn't touched another human being in almost a year.

Still, we're going to watch *Carrie* tonight. We started watching horror films together over a year ago when I was still avoiding how I felt about Mum being ill. One night I dragged my numbness over to Heather's flat and sat crouched in the corner of her kitchen on the stepstool she uses to reach the high shelves while she cooked for us. After dinner we put on some proper scary old-school slasher and it turned out to be the perfect catharsis for a lot of angry emotions I didn't realize I had.

Since then, we've both become convinced of the healing power of horror. We've established a semi-regular fright night and now that we can't be in the same room, we synchronize our start times and keep up a running text commentary as we watch. Of course, all the Grand Guignol is considerably less terrifying when you're scrolling through your phone looking for the dripping-dagger emoji but that's no bad thing. Without the soothing effect of second-screening I'd never have made it to the end of *The Babadook*.

There were a lot of these rituals when the virus first bloomed. I paused work every morning for virtual elevenses with Nicola, and Heather usually joined us later in the day for after-work beero-zeros, which was Nicola's name for the alcohol-free lagers she was drinking during her pregnancy. Once a fortnight, I corralled the whole gang – Neil, Bledi, Tessa and the rest – for a Saturday

morning second breakfast. Marisa and the girls had a standing date for Sunday afternoon quarantinis, a term that still turns my brother-in-law purple with cynicism. I would have gagged at it once, too.

But it was lovely, the way everyone kept making time for each other, the way we made the effort. Not all of our new customs stuck around and it's probably for the best, since working and socializing entirely on screen takes its toll on your eyes as much as your brain. But I do understand now, in a way I never expected to, how committed my friends are to me and I to them. Laura and I have chatted more in the past six months than we have in the past six years; Ben and John are constantly checking on how I'm doing and are always on hand for a late-night whisky.

It's 2pm, which is when I play cards with Genny. I press the icon with the camera on it and Skype plays its jaunty, seesawing ringtone, the notes anticipating the beat and urging the person at the other end to hurry up and get to the call. Genny's usually there fairly quickly. She's expecting me and, anyway, her apartment's not that large.

'Well good *morning*,' she says, as if she's happily surprised to hear from me, as if we don't do this every day. 'And how are you today?' Her Southern vowels make everything she says sound richer, plumper, more pleasant.

I met Genny on my debut solo trip to North Carolina;

she was good friends with the elderly couple who first took me in. Genny lives in a backwater town halfway between the big city and the mountains and we met up a few times, whenever I was passing through, and always enjoyed each other's company. Genny had an enthusiasm, curiosity and verve that was not at all what I expected of a long-retired woman living alone in a small rural community whose best days were long behind it.

'Morning!' I say, in deference to the five-hour time difference. The dark blank box on my screen switches to colour and resolves into a pixelly outline of a head and shoulders. Genny's PC is fairly ancient and Lord only knows what the broadband's like out there in the boondocks. It always takes a moment before her curly crop of diamond-white hair shifts into focus. She is still wearing her pyjamas. As am I.

'I'm just bringing up the cards,' she says. This usually takes a good minute or two – I swear she's using Netscape – and at some stage my screen will suddenly fill with the torso and haunches of a large feline, who has leaped onto her desk and taken up a sentry position across the keyboard. Genny's cat Alice has never trusted the talking vision that appears to her mistress daily. She will be carried out of the bedroom then bribed with treats to stop her scratching at the closed door.

Genny was one of the people on my list at the start of

lockdown. I knew she wouldn't lack for conversation – her family and friends phone her often – but I did worry about how bored she might be, with nowhere to go and no one to see. So I found a really simple website with a virtual card table and we started playing the only game we both knew, which was rummy. Goodness knows how many hundreds of hands we've played now, although I could probably work it out since we get through three a day.

We ask each other what we did yesterday. It's always a pretty short list. Genny washed some sheets. I did some writing. Sometimes we discuss the news and whether it's worse in her country or mine. Politics isn't something Genny likes to discuss, although she sometimes sighs about 'the terrible things happening here', and I know she means Trump.

We often swap book recommendations; Genny has always loved reading and it's one of the things we first bonded over. Her age makes her vulnerable to the virus so she can't visit the shops but the local library is operating a drive-thru system and every few days she turns up and asks the young folk at the window-counter to find her something new. She lets them choose – that way, she says, she'll learn something she didn't expect to – and they wipe the covers down for her and stick them in the trunk of her car. Last week it was a biography of Steve Jobs. She told me it was very interesting but she didn't much like the sound

of him, whatever he may have achieved with computers.

When Genny was growing up, in the thirties and forties, books were her escape. Her family lived on a farm in upcountry South Carolina where they grew everything they ate, ate everything they grew and pickled whatever they could for the winter. Books didn't just fuel her imagination; they showed her that a different life was possible.

She was the only one of several siblings not to marry early, settle down and spend her youth making house and babies for a man from the next county. With extraordinary boldness, she moved to a big city, learned bookkeeping and rented her own flat. She enjoyed her independence, had a few men friends and fell in love with a young man who went to the Korean War and never came back. It took me several years to discover all this about her because Genny is far more interested in listening to other people than talking about herself.

Whenever I stayed with her, she always wanted to hear about my travels, where I was going, what I was up to. She said she loved the sound of my adventures and I said, well why don't you come with me on one? So we took a ten-day road trip around South Carolina and Georgia and confused every waiter, receptionist and taxi driver we came across. 'Are y'all related?' they always asked us, thrown by the collision of accents, and we'd say no and

you could see their consternation as they tried and failed to fathom a relationship between the eighty-something Southern lady and the British companion half her age.

It was on that trip I found out how many times she'd been proposed to, which was three more than me. She accepted, once, because she was in her twenties and all her friends were doing it. And then one day, she met up with her fiancé for a meal and said quite candidly that he was a very good friend but she didn't feel ready to get married, and he looked a little relieved and said he didn't want to get married either, and they left it at that.

I know she hasn't given up on the thought of male companionship, or even love. She's a very sociable woman, as bartenders have discovered whenever we've been out together. She finds it easy to make conversation and friends, and since our road trip, she's mentioned a couple of coffee shops she's noticed in neighbouring towns, places that have a mature clientele, where she might sit with a book and talk to a few nice men. I love her chutzpah. I love to think that I might have helped reignite it.

'Well, did you ever see anything like it?' says Genny, as she beats me in all three of our games. I tell her she's the world champion.

Before the pandemic started to get serious I decamped to my sister's for a while. Usually I laugh at Kate for being an

CHAPTER 13

overworrier but for once I could see the value in it. She'd
been worrying since the middle of January, so she had a
head start on the rest of us.

In February, when I had to travel to Sweden, she made
me promise that I wouldn't touch anything in the airport
and that I'd wipe down my cutlery before I ate. She also
asked me to check if the shops in Stockholm still had hand
sanitizer. They didn't.

Kate suggested that I move in with her and Justin
before – as she seemed to think likely – the UK's capital
was sealed off from the rest of the country and left to fester
in its own plaguey air. I said I was fine but a week later she
asked again and her insistence was pretty touching. When
I eventually agreed, she sent Justin over to pick me up in
the old Jeep he uses for his bar business and we stuffed it
with my spare mattress, a suitcase with a month's worth
of clothes, some cardboard boxes full of pasta and tinned
beans, and a couple of nine-packs of loo roll. It looked like
we were heading to a festival.

This wasn't exactly how I'd imagined the apocalypse
but the empty shelves in the shops were unnerving me.
I recognized them from a lifetime of watching zombie
movies; societal breakdown seemed only a couple of
frames away. Soon people would be roaming the streets
with improvized weapons and riding trolleys through
deserted shopping centres. I, meanwhile, would be

rubbish at defending myself. I'd gone clay pigeon shooting with Dad once and I hadn't hit a single thing.

Justin laughed at the extent of my existential dread but he also hugged me when I cried and told me everything was going to be fine. I'm grateful, obviously, that it wasn't the end of the world but I'm also grateful to know that there are people who have got my back. At the moment we pulled away from the kerb, my phone flashed up a text message from Kate that just said, 'See you at the Burrow, Hermione!' and I thought that moment might be the most loved I've ever felt.

Even at my sister's house, though, there were parts of my brain and my adrenal system that took a while to feel safe. A lot of nights I couldn't sleep – or, more often, I couldn't stay asleep because I kept shocking myself awake in the middle of nightmares. One night, I was sure I heard a scream of engines overhead and lay in bed paralyzed by the thought that I'd just heard the first air strike of an imminent world war.

In the end, the cure for my anxiety was simply being an aunt. We couldn't discuss the frightening prospect of a deadly virus, an overwhelmed health service and a crashing economy around a nearly four year old, at least not one who was smart enough to operate an iPad. Izzy had more important things she needed to talk to me about anyway, like where we were going to build a den next,

which *Moana* songs I knew the words to and who was my favourite Fraggle.

She required a *lot* of entertainment. We had dance parties in the sitting room and PE in the garden, and every day it didn't rain I took her hand and walked her down the road to a little public space that was full of daffodils and apple trees where we played hide and seek and collected daisies to leave out for the fairies. Sometimes she looked up at me gravely and told me 'I'm glad you're here,' and at least once a day I'd receive some spontaneous display of affection – a breathless hug, a half-squashed dandelion or a piece of colouring in. It has always amazed me how often, unprompted, she will tell me she loves me. It never gets old.

Still, when the restrictions lifted a little, I moved back to the city. Sleeping in an attic, on a mattress on the floor, had started feeling a bit Victorian governess-y, a little close to the bone. I'm not ready to see myself as an adjunct to other people's lives: my sister's sister, my niece's aunt, my father's daughter. It's OK for a while and then I need my autonomy and the space to be myself.

Also, I need to be somewhere I can eat an entire packet of custard creams and not feel guilty about it.

I haven't been lonely in my flat, not really. The solitude isn't a problem; I handle it well. I call my friends, I do my

work, I lose myself in long, involved TV series, sometimes I even read a book and remember how clever it makes me feel. For company, I turn on the radio or listen to a podcast. If I need a shot in the arm, I blast a Beatles album through the speakers and sing loudly along. This isn't the first time I've been alone for extended periods and these are all things I know work for me.

I've probably been in training for this crisis my entire single life.

When I ask my girlfriends if they're lonely, they also say no. Not lonely, says Heather, just bored. Not lonely, says Tessa, just fed up. Not lonely, says Alex, just – y'know – missing people. We're all getting by and sometimes it's better and sometimes it's worse.

One of the things isolation seems to have revealed is how many different shades of emotional grey exist, from just-about-OK to slightly-sub-par to barely-hanging-in-there. It's amazing to think back a few months, to the myriad ways we harnessed our nervous energy, and the relief of escaping armageddon. We organized, we exercised, we therapized. Marisa crocheted, Nicola knitted, Tessa bought power weights and got really hench. I finally downloaded a meditation app. For a short while, we laughed in the face of our landlocked status. We turned it into a superstrength.

Then our reserves ran dry and our vigour began to

dwindle. We were like sailors caught in the doldrums, stranded in the middle of an utterly becalmed sea. And now there are days when I can't remember what it feels like to be me, the real me, the one who gets excited and gets loud and gets tears in her eyes when she laughs too hard. I know there must be ways to summon her but they feel like ancient ways. The ritual's been lost and the artefacts have gone missing and no one quite remembers how to articulate the spell.

Then there are the days when I don't feel much like a person at all and (or is it because?) there's no one around to prove otherwise. If those days begin to accumulate, I've noticed, I become less likely to reach out to my friends rather than more. I sink further into my couch and watch more and more telly until I feel I'm literally rotting inside, like a big piece of fermenting fruit that's eventually just going to fill up with rotten gases and explode. I'm not sure what the technical definition for that is.

Perhaps I'd call it a perfectly reasonable glimpse of insanity. The natural and almost inevitable reaction to an extreme lack of human contact. Still, I don't think I'd call it loneliness. I don't think I've had a lot of experience with loneliness in my life at all. For all the powerful sensations my singleness has induced – embarrassment, emancipation, unnaturalness, inferiority, superiority – it has rarely beleaguered me with loneliness.

And even when it has, the times I have felt most lonely have rarely been ones where I was completely alone. It's an emotion that's skewered me at the oddest times. Like at a work do where people's partners are invited along and suddenly the sphere in which I most belong no longer feels like mine. Or the moment a really great night out is ending and everyone is saying goodbye and about to head off in pairs.

There was, of course, the time I bought two tickets to a sold-out play and I couldn't find anyone who wanted to go with me. I tried to return the second ticket but I'd left it too late. So I went on my own because I really wanted to see the show, which I'd purposely not read about to avoid spoilers, and five minutes before the curtain went up this thousand-seater auditorium was buzzing with anticipation; every single seat was taken except the one next to me and everyone was talking excitedly to the person they'd come with, except for me. And it turned out the play was a one-man show about loneliness. It didn't even have a happy ending.

But that was an extreme case.

Usually I don't *experience* loneliness as much as fear it. That's its power over me. It's the bogeyman that lies in wait for little girls who get distracted on their way through the woods. It's the fairy-tale punishment that awaits me if I don't wish hard enough for my Prince Charming. It's

the inevitable outcome for anyone who fails to create a miniature replica of themselves to love them and look after them in old age.

I supposed that's why I can't help feeling afraid and sorry for my future self, even when my present self is doing just fine. I've been so primed to feel anxiety about being single – so indoctrinated with the belief that everyone else's way of doing things is more comforting and rewarding– that I forget to notice that my life has, to date, proven all those fears wrong.

And that's crazy. Because even in a proto-apocalypse, I've never had more people to love.

I think I'll cycle over to Tessa's house before it gets too dark. I can't go inside but I can stand on her drive and we can chat through the doorway. I know it's freezing out but I can wear the really thick coat I bought a couple of years ago, when I had to travel to Maine and Vermont in the middle of winter. Maybe the snow boots too.

I've thought a lot about my travels since we've all been permanently grounded. The images of them flit through my mind without prompting, which is weird, because that never used to happen. It used to be a frustration of mine, the fact that I'd had all these experiences and yet never spent time remembering them or reflecting on them or appreciating them. Since lockdown, I haven't even had

to try – it's like they're *desperate* to get out. Little bursts of memory from a secret store, freeze-dried happiness from a survivalist bunker I didn't know I'd built.

I guess I've always tended to look forward rather than back. I've been fixated on the single life as one of opportunity and possibility, the idea that I can go and do and be whatever I want, and fill my life with a breadth of experiences that will be the envy of all. Maybe I don't reflect so much on the things I've already done, the person I already am.

I have an Australian cousin, Jennifer. I think we're very alike. She lived in London for most of her twenties and thirties. When she first arrived, she stayed on my couch and worked as a nanny, and spent every penny and every weekend travelling to the European continent to see a new country. She'd grown up in a fairly remote part of Queensland and the fact that you could cross so many international borders in the time it would take her parents to get to the next big town had really motivated her.

We're still close, even now she's back home. She's been living alone in an apartment in Brisbane and I know that when she first moved there she missed the UK and her friends here, so we've been FaceTiming and WhatsApping and the rest. The other day, she told me something really unexpected. She said she reckons lockdown's been really good for her because before it came along, she was

going out every night and filling her time with too many activities. 'I've had time to pause and reflect and realize that it's OK when I stay at home and not do very much,' she said. 'That's really good for me to know.'

There are a number of epiphanies happening among my friends. We've noticed what we really miss and what, it turns out, we can happily do without. Robin, who had often told herself she could never work from home because she needed the daily social interaction of the office, has decided she is both more productive and more zen, and she'll never go back. She also discovered it made her furious when the first thing the government reopened was the department stores. 'I don't need to *shop* right now,' she said, 'I need to see *art*!'

I, meanwhile, am surprised to find myself rejoicing that I no longer have to hug people I barely know. I've always thought of myself as a really tactile person but I've realized I only actually want to get touchy-feely with the people I care about and I deeply resent the awkward and unwanted lurch-and-pat you get from friends of friends. Or the excruciating facial proximity of the double air kiss that is, for some reason, considered a sophisticated way to greet people you've never met before.

I've never had a problem with a good old handshake but since that too is probably consigned to history, I hope that, post-Covid, we'll be adopting a smile and a nod of

the head instead, and I cheer for the fact that it will no longer be socially acceptable for strangers to lunge into my personal space without my permission.

Tessa has told me, in the past, that one of the advantages of being single over coupledom is that you get to know yourself better. 'We're so lucky not to have to compromise who we are or define ourselves through someone else,' she says. I've always slightly resisted this idea because it seems to me that I'd be a better person if I had someone to reflect me back to myself and who was happy to tell me when I was being a dick. Honestly, there aren't many friends who'll do that for you. Maybe when I get to Tessa's I can ask her to tell me some of my most dickish traits and then I can work on them.

I'm actually looking forward to seeing her already. I think that's one of the things I like most about lockdown, how any opportunity to see a friend is sacred. I even love the Zoom calls, still, after a year. I know it's because I don't have to do a lot of them for work and it's different for people who have lots of online meetings, who get Zoom fatigue. Very often before one of our meet-ups, there's a last-minute apology from someone who's suddenly realized they can't face it, who says they're sorry but they just need to close their screen and have a lie down. In the old days, I think I'd have been a little offended but I'm not now. I've learned that you've just gotta do what you've gotta do.

And anyway, when my friends flash up on my screen in a grid of windows, it makes me appreciate my relationships in a different way. Here we are, stacked up next to each other like shipping containers, each restricted to our own frame, none of us able to reach beyond it. Maybe our confinement ought to make us sad but isn't it really just being human?

I think of my friends' resilience, and I think of Genny, of her extraordinary life, and the woman she is. And future loneliness doesn't frighten me so much any more.

CHAPTER 14

The word spinster can still make me wince. But now I wonder whether it's just the word I feel defensive about – its notes of fustiness and desiccation, of lavender soap and lace-edged hankies – or something more.

I've been an unmarried single woman for two decades now. I'm not just a member of that club, I'm a senior one – the kind who's running the bar and doing a reluctant stint as secretary too. I shouldn't need to be told it's OK to be single. Feminism already won that battle. But you can't dissolve a couple of millennia of human behaviour overnight. The perception of women as more than just wives and mothers has barely been current for half a century. Not every external marker or internal barometer has caught up with the rapid change society has undergone.

So maybe it's no wonder that there's some cognitive dissonance in the way I feel about being single – that I'm overcome not just with a visceral embarrassment at admitting to it but a matching guilt for feeling any shame at all.

Maybe it's hard to embrace single life when you've always got one eye on the future hope or current absence of a partner in your life.

Or maybe it's not hard but we think it should be.

Maybe it's all of these things.

The last time I stayed with Kate and Justin, Izzy came in early one morning to bounce on my mattress – it was, she said, a lot bouncier than hers, which made it more fun. And after she had been throwing herself around for a while with an energy I could only admire, even while I wished she'd left me asleep, she paused to make an observation.

'Emma,' she said, 'this is your bed, isn't it?'

'Yes,' I said.

'But you've got a bed in London, too?'

'Yes,' I said.

'And one at Nana and Grandad's?'

'Yes,' I said.

Izzy frowned and considered this.

'You've got a lot of beds.'

She had a point. Just look at all the many spare rooms in which I'd made myself temporarily at home. I thought of Genny and Susan, and all the strangers-turned-friends who had taken me in and made me part of their family. I seemed to have a habit, or a talent, for grafting myself onto other people's lives, sometimes for a few days, sometimes for months.

Oh God, was I some sort of parasitic plant?

These are the kinds of things I ask myself. If I had a

partner, of course, I'd have said it out loud and maybe my partner would have laughed and said, 'Of *course* not,' and pulled me into a big hug and told me how great I was. Or maybe he'd have pulled a face and said, 'Yes, you're like that giant red flower that grows in the jungle and stinks of rotting meat,' because he's sarcastic and for some reason he really knows his botany. Either way, I'd probably have got some sort of response and moved on.

Instead the question was trapped in my brain and hung around for ages until I remembered that I was still good friends with all of these people I'd lived with and most of them had invited me back. Clearly I wasn't unwanted. Clearly my presence offered something in return: an infusion of new conversation and perspectives, a change of pace from their normal routine, a little light relief, perhaps. I wasn't parasitic, I decided, I was symbiotic, like those mushrooms that hang around at the bottom of big trees, putting nutrients back into the soil.

And then it occurred to me that I didn't have to see myself as a humble little mushroom. Maybe I was a tree too, just a different kind of tree. Not the regular kind with a big thick trunk and a neat geometric shape but one of those messy-looking ones with roots that drop down from their branches and spread themselves all over the place. A banyan tree, whose dangling roots can grow so strong that they prop it up as it carries on expanding, seeking out new

ground. Soon you can't even tell which is its central trunk. It doesn't matter to the tree. The tree is getting everything it needs.

The people I have loved and the places I have been and the events I have encountered have not been a substitute for something else. My experience has been full and entire, just as I am full and entire. I haven't lived a life defined by absence and I won't spend the rest of it waiting on a future invisible.

So what *does* happy ever after look like if your prince never shows up? This is a question I have never really asked myself before. For me, single life was supposed to be a glorious *rumspringa*, a chance to ride every rollercoaster in the park before the Big Settle Down. A limbo life, but a happy one – a holding pattern filled with infinitely entertaining distractions.

I suppose if I were trying to sell singleness, trying to pitch it as the dream ending to my story, I'd focus on the aspirational stuff.

You'll probably age better, I'd say. You'll wrinkle slower. Think of all those hours of sleep you've already got on the rest of humanity, all the nights no partner or child has kicked or shaken you awake. Think of all those eight-hour stretches of luxurious slumber still to come and the unending rota of other people's hassles that you won't wake up to.

Your holidays will better. You *know* they will. No compromise destinations, no make-the-best-of-it camping, no hours of enforced boredom sat in the freezing café of a soft-play centre.

You'll meet lots of people and have the opportunity to get to know them, to make as many friends as you want. You won't be hamstrung by your partner's reluctance to go out or the complex tapestry of the kids' extracurricular activities. You won't have to make do with the slightly unsettling couple you met at the school gates or the people you already see way too much of at work.

You'll never have to feel guilty about fancying someone. (There may be a few caveats to this.)

You'll have more disposable income. Well you would, anyway, if you got a real job.

All of these benefits have, at some time or other, made me happy to be single. I do worry, though, that there's something disingenuous about them. They sound like compensation, not the thing itself. They don't add up to a life.

The problem with making the case for single living is that we have to define it by the thing it isn't. And it's always single people who lose out in that comparison, not the other way round. It's easy to list the experiences we lack, but partnering up and parenting involve relinquishment too.

I remember – when I was younger and coupled life seemed so much more sophisticated than my own – envying other people's weekends. Those indolent lie-ins in suggestively rumpled sheets, breakfast on a tray, choosing something fun to do with the rest of the day. It took me far too long to realize that couples didn't have a patent on lazy Sundays. And now my friends with children have to barter with each other for the right to stay in bed.

Being with someone else demands sacrifice – not just of your time, or your resources, or your long-held dreams, but of parts of yourself, parts that you'll never notice, never become. And the joy of being single isn't in filling your life with compensatory excitements, or gloating over your independence. It's in being the truest and most complete version of yourself that will ever exist.

I can't deny that I'd like a little reassurance on the journey. I'm human; I need security, stability, a sense of home. I'd like the same safety I felt, for a time, with Matt. The things that the prince, and the palace, and the brood of princelets are supposed to deliver.

Sometimes it's hard to see where that's coming from, although more often, it's hard to appreciate where it already exists. It's difficult to create a language for it when all the vocabulary for grown-up contentment belongs to coupledom. How do you 'make a home' on your own? Or 'build a life' without kids? Can you 'settle down' when the

people closest to you keep making decisions without you, and moving away?

It feels like I'm trying to make a garden out of Lego but the pieces I've got are for an industrial military base and half of them are missing. There are no instructions and the picture on the lid of the box shows nothing but a miserable-looking gardener holding a cat.

There's an asterisk next to the cat. The accompanying text says 'Cat not included'.

I didn't choose singleness, not in the way that other people choose to live with each other, or to marry, or even to divorce. But I *have* chosen independence, a life without compromise, a future of my own making.

What will that future look like? I think a little like this.

I will live in my flat in London, for a while, at least. I will decide to redecorate, to make it feel new, only this time I'll pay a professional and when they're finished the rooms will look more grown-up and just a bit luxurious. The record player will still belt out Beatles songs and the fridge will still be stocked with wine and beer. But I'll cook a little more expansively for myself, use some of the recipes I made for Dad, learn some more. I'll even bake.

I will travel home to my parents' house at the weekends and Kate, Justin, Izzy, Ethan and I will sit in the garden and picnic, even if it's cold, and our parents will sit on the

patio behind the clear plastic sheeting that Dad has erected to keep them safe. We'll learn to raise our voices to the right volume to have a normal conversation through the plastic and Izzy will play on her old swing set. She'll find toys she'd forgotten about in the Wendy house and want to show them to us one by one. She will not let her little brother touch them, even though they're too young for her now, because they're *hers*.

And after an hour or two of sharing news about preschool and hospital visits and the new cabinet I've bought for my living room, we'll pack up to go and, just as we're waving goodbye, Izzy will run up to the plastic barrier and stick her face against it, and Mum and Dad will both lean down to give her a kiss from the other side.

And when this crisis is over, the plastic sheeting will be gone and we will all sit down to Sunday lunch. Ethan will cry a little at first when Mum holds him, but then she'll sing him a silly song with made-up lyrics and he'll break out in his killer-handsome smile.

I'll watch horror movies with Heather, eat pie with the girls, go to the pub with the guys. Nicola and Alistair will move to the suburbs to bring up their baby. It will hurt more than I expected to see them go and for a short while I'll be freaked out, afraid that our little community won't survive their departure. But I'll understand that I haven't been abandoned, that I'm no less loved.

I'll travel less because I'm trying to learn the lessons of lockdown and climate change and become a more responsible person. It will occur to me, finally, that I could do worse than turn my curiosity and eagerness to connect on the people who live closer to home. I'll wonder if there's some sort of job that could use those skills in a good cause. Maybe I'll even find one.

I will recognize my own resilience and learn to see the person I live with every day in all her moods and colours, and to love them each a bit better.

I'll cycle through my local streets and be reminded that there are many attractive men in this city. And that some of them may even be single.

I'll go for drives in Aggie and take long walks with my father and realize how deeply I love the countryside. Maybe one day I may even move there and get a dog.

But for now, I'll start by sleeping in the middle of my own bed.

ACKNOWLEDGEMENTS

It would have been impossible to tackle any of the topics in this book without the support of my friends and my family. I'm so grateful to everyone who let me share stories, and in a number of places I've changed their names or details, because it was the right thing to do. To all those who helped me tease out my thoughts, who untangled my memories and offered their own, I offer both thanks and my enduring love: Marisa, Becki, Nicola, Luffers, Jo, Neil, Alex, Karen, Jenny, Genny and cousin Jen, Ben and John and both the Sarahs. T-Boz gets a special mention for the many times she let me think aloud to her on long lockdown phone calls.

I am indebted to my sympathetic, generous and brilliantly perceptive editor Romilly Morgan for guiding me through difficult subjects and a turbulent year; and I'm grateful to Faye Robson, Megan Brown and Hazel O'Brien at Octopus for all their kindnesses. Huge thanks to Cathryn Summerhayes and Jess Molloy, my champions at Curtis Brown, for bringing me under their wing(s). And to my family, who have borne the brunt of my bookwriting moods three times now – thank you for still loving me, and for always giving me a home.